DELTA TEACHER DEVELOPMENT SERIES

Series editors Mike Burghall and Lindsay Clandfield

Teaching Unplugged

Dogme in English Language Teaching

Luke Meddings and Scott Thornbury

DELTA PUBLISHING

Published by
DELTA PUBLISHING
Quince Cottage
Hoe Lane
Peaslake
Surrey GU5 9SW
England

www.deltapublishing.co.uk

© Delta Publishing 2009

First published 2009
Reprinted 2010, 2012

ISBN 978-1-905085-19-4

Edited by Mike Burghall
Designed by Christine Cox
Cover photo © iStockphoto.com/Alexander Hafemann
Printed in Greece by Bakis

Acknowledgements

Dogme has always been a collaborative, jointly-constructed
experience, and the authors wish to express their sincere
thanks to all the contributors to the Dogme discussion
group who, over the years, have nurtured and shaped its
development, both affirming and challenging its core
principles, and fleshing these out with inspired practical
applications.

It would be invidious to single out names, but special thanks
are due to Rob Haines for – among other things – his helpful
input on Part A of *Teaching Unplugged*.

Luke would also like to thank John McKenzie, David King,
Jack Bovill, Louis Alexander and Jimmy Leach for their
encouragement and interest in new teaching ideas over the
years; and his friend Neil, sister Tamsin, wife Sylwia and
children Zaki and Marina for retaining an interest in him.

Both authors also owe an enormous debt of gratitude to the
editorial team at Delta, and especially to Lindsay Clandfield
and Mike Burghall, and designer Christine Cox, for their
undiminished enthusiasm for and commitment to this
project.

Scott would like to dedicate this book to the memory of his
grandfather, Conway Burgess, 'an inspired and visionary
teacher'.

Luke would like to dedicate the book to two lovers of
language, Tom and Pauline Meddings.

From the authors

Scott's story

In 2000 I was working as a teacher trainer in Spain. My colleagues and I were becoming increasingly frustrated with what appeared to be the prevailing orthodoxy in second language teaching, one in which the people in the room were somehow incidental to the process of teaching, where the learners were simply frogmarched down a one-way grammar street, or where the lesson space was filled to overflowing with *activities*, at the expense of the learning *opportunities*. And this was despite the lip-service paid by their teachers to a 'communicative' approach.

To a large extent, the problem seemed to stem from an over-reliance on materials and technological aids. Classroom interactions were being mediated almost entirely through 'imported' texts. Lack of engagement with such texts, and the activities they generated, meant that learners were interacting at the lowest level of involvement – like car engines that are 'idling' but not going anywhere.

Accordingly, we instituted a rather draconian policy whereby materials were to be used minimally and judiciously. On our training courses, we recorded segments of lesson talk and analysed them from the perspective of the communication displayed. The improvement in the quality of the teaching was dramatic.

When, around the same time and by chance, I went to see a Dogme film and read the Dogme 95 manifesto, I found a metaphor for the kind of teaching that we were aiming at. The first 'vow' of a Dogme film-maker is:

> *Shooting should be done on location. Props and sets must not be brought in (if a particular prop is necessary for the story, a location must be chosen where the prop is to be found).*

I then wrote an article suggesting that ELT needed a similar 'rescue action'. I called it Dogme ELT, the first commandment of which began:

> *Teaching should be done using only the resources that teachers and students bring to the classroom – ie themselves – and whatever happens to be in the classroom.*

The uptake was instant, surprising and gratifying. Before long, enough people (including Luke) had got in touch to justify starting a web-based discussion group.

Scott

Luke's story

Around the time Scott and his colleagues were re-evaluating their teacher training course in Barcelona, I was helping to set up an experimental language school in London.

Working as a journalist in ELT, I had grown tired of hearing about 'optimum course delivery', as if language were a 'product' and learning a 'package'. My years as a teacher suggested that that a worthwhile lesson was an *experience*: vital, unrepeatable, and brought to life by the spontaneous interaction between learners and teacher. I was determined that the new school should reflect this, and took with me two books that had set me thinking.

One was the Common European Framework of Reference for Modern Languages. I liked its summary of what language learning should be for:

> *'to satisfy … communicative needs'*, enabling learners to *'exchange information and ideas … and communicate their thoughts and feelings'*.

To communicate thoughts and feelings! By the 1990s one might have been forgiven for thinking that language learning was all about grammar and accuracy. Coursebooks were colourful and full of pictures of celebrities, but it was as if we had regressed to the era of grammar translation.

The second book was a copy of *The Future of English?* by David Graddol. I was particularly struck by his prediction of a bilingual future, in which 'authority' would pass from mono-lingual to bi-lingual or multi-lingual speakers of English.

Our new students were coming to us with their English, not coming to us *for* English. They belonged to a world in which English was being used and taught more widely than ever before: they were Graddol's new generation, for whom English was simply *there*, in one form or another, *in the world*.

What they wanted was to engage with it. Our first courses were conversation-based and used no coursebook. Bring your English, we said, and we'll build on it together.

It proved hard to sustain this simple model as the school grew. I felt isolated, which is why Scott's article in *IATEFL Issues* made such an impact. Like many others reading it, or subsequently joining the discussion group, I realised I wasn't alone.

Luke

Contents

Contents

TEACHING
UNPLUGGED

Dogme 95:
A filmmaking movement set up by a group of
Danish filmmakers who challenged what they
saw as cinema's dependency on special effects,
technical wizardry and fantasy. The emphasis
on the here-and-now requires the filmmaker to
focus on the actual story and its relevance to
the audience.

Dogme ELT:
A teaching movement set up by a group of
English teachers who challenge what they
consider to be an over-reliance on materials and
technical wizardry in current language teaching.
The emphasis on the here-and-now requires the
teacher to focus on the actual learners and the
content that is relevant to them.

Teaching unplugged

Many language teachers have expressed a wish to free themselves from a dependency on materials, aids and technology, and to work with nothing more than the 'raw materials' provided by the people in the room. Or, in other words, to 'unplug' their teaching.

The beliefs and practices embodied in what is known as the Dogme ELT philosophy offer the ways and means to do exactly this. These beliefs and practices, in turn, draw on a rich tradition of alternative, progressive, critical, and humanist educational theory. To give you a flavour, here are five quotations from a variety of sources:

- *Education is communication and dialogue. It is not the transference of knowledge.* (Paulo Freire, Brazilian educationalist and author of 'Pedagogy of the Oppressed')
- *The only questions asked in a school should be by the pupils.* (A. S. Neill, founder of the progressive school 'Summerhill')
- *Success depends less on materials, techniques and linguistic analyses, and more on what goes on inside and between the people in the classroom.* (Earl Stevick, humanist English language teacher and thinker)
- *To most truly teach, one must converse; to truly converse is to teach.* (Roland Tharp and Ronald Gallimore, reforming educationalists and authors of 'Rousing Minds to Life')
- *A good teacher cannot be fixed in a routine … . During teaching, each moment requires a sensitive mind that is constantly changing and constantly adapting.* (Bruce Lee, kung fu practitioner and film star)

The Dogme philosophy grew out of ideas and beliefs about language teaching that echo many of the sentiments in the quotations above.

Dogme in ELT

Since its inception in March 2000, the Dogme discussion list provided the forum where these ideas and beliefs were debated, challenged, adapted, and exemplified. Out of this 'long conversation' emerged ten key principles, each tagged to a key word, that characterise a Dogme approach:

- Materials-mediated teaching is the 'scenic' route to learning, but the direct route is located in the **interactivity** between teachers and learners, and between the learners themselves.
- The content most likely to **engage** learners and to trigger learning processes is that which is already there, supplied by 'the people in the room'.

'The importance of
interaction is not simply
that it creates learning
opportunities, it is that it
constitutes learning itself.'
Dick Allwright [1]

- Learning is a social and *dialogic* process, where knowledge is co-constructed rather than 'transmitted' or 'imported' from teacher/coursebook to learner.
- Learning can be mediated through talk, especially talk that is shaped and supported (ie *scaffolded*) by the teacher.
- Rather than being acquired, language (including grammar) *emerges*: it is an organic process that occurs given the right conditions.
- The teacher's primary function, apart from promoting the kind of classroom dynamic which is conducive to a dialogic and emergent pedagogy, is to optimise language learning *affordances*, by, for example, directing attention to features of the emergent language.
- Providing space for the learner's *voice* means accepting that the learner's beliefs, knowledge, experiences, concerns and desires are valid content in the language classroom.
- Freeing the classroom from third-party, imported materials *empowers* both teachers and learners.
- Texts, when used, should have *relevance* for the learner, in both their learning and using contexts.
- Teachers and learners need to unpack the ideological baggage associated with English Language Teaching materials – to become *critical* users of such texts.

Of these ten principles, three core precepts stand out:

- Dogme is about teaching that is *conversation-driven*.
- Dogme is about teaching that is *materials-light*.
- Dogme is about teaching that *focuses on emergent language*.

Let's look at these three precepts in more detail, and in so doing lay the foundations for the practical classroom procedures and activities that realise a Dogme approach: an unplugged approach.

1 Conversation-driven

There are at least five reasons why conversation should occupy a key role in language learning. These are:

- Conversation is language at work.
- Conversation is discourse.
- Conversation is interactive, dialogic and communicative.
- Conversation scaffolds learning.
- Conversation promotes socialisation.

Let's look at each of these points in turn.

'The confusions which
occupy us arise when
language is like an
engine idling, not when
it is doing its work.'
Ludwig Wittgenstein [3]

Conversation is language at work

Conversation is the fundamental, universal and default form of language. In the words of one linguist, it is 'the most basic and widespread linguistic means of conducting human affairs'. [2] For this reason, most language learners feel cheated if their course includes little or no conversation practice. Hence, most language learning methods have prioritised the teaching of the spoken language. However, conventionally, conversation is viewed as the *product* of learning: that is, learners first have to master the grammar and vocabulary before they are allowed to apply this knowledge in fluency activities. This means that, in being left to last, conversation is often neglected. Also, it is less easily 'testable' than knowledge of grammar and vocabulary, and it is often the case that what is not tested will not be taught.

More importantly, to move from grammatical accuracy to conversational fluency is to move in exactly the opposite direction from the way that naturalistic language learning occurs. In first language learning, the ability to participate in 'proto-conversations' with parents or siblings is a skill that pre-dates, by years, the acquisition of an adult-like grammar and vocabulary. In fact, some researchers are of the opinion that conversation is not so much *evidence* of grammatical acquisition, but a pre-requisite for it. As Evelyn Hatch puts it:

> *Our basic premise has long been that the child learns some basic set of syntactic structures, moving from a one-word phase to a two-word phase, to more complex structures, and that eventually the child is able to put these structures together in order to carry on conversations with others. The premise, if we use discourse analysis, is the converse. That is, language learning evolves out of learning how to carry on conversations.* [4]

Hatch is, of course, talking about the learning of a first language, and it is always dangerous to attempt to draw parallels between first and second language acquisition. Nevertheless, evidence from studies of second language learning in naturalistic (ie non-classroom) situations seems to support the view that – at least for learners who have plentiful speaking opportunities – a 'fluency-first' approach works well. This, of course, is a key principle of *task-based learning*. In a task-based approach, the teaching-learning cycle starts with a fluency activity, and the learner's production forms the raw material for subsequent language-focused work. In fact, a Dogme approach shares many of the beliefs and features of a task-based approach.

Conversation is discourse

Discourse is the use to which language is put in order to fulfil the specific communicative needs of its users in specific contexts. Typically, discourse is sustained over several turns (of talk) or sentences (of text). Thus, engaging in conversation involves a lot more than the stacking of isolated sentences one on top of the other. In conversations, speakers co-operate in order to jointly construct a discourse that is both connected and coherent. Speakers respond to, and build on, successive utterances, while at the same time ensuring (and expecting) that whatever is said will be somehow relevant, both to what has been said before and to the immediate context.

Arguments in favour of taking a discourse-level view of language (rather than a sentence-level or an utterance-level view) have gained currency in the last few decades, not least because of the common-sense understanding that all real-life language use occurs as discourse. Hence, the capacity to understand and produce isolated sentences is of limited applicability to real-life language use.

Nevertheless, language teaching has – for a long time – focused primarily on the sentence, rather than on the text, as the basic unit of language. Language teaching traditionally starts (and often ends) with the analysis and production of sentence-level grammatical features, such as verb tenses. An approach that foregrounds larger stretches of language, such as connected talk, might be better preparation for real-life language use. That, at least, is the argument of the Dogme approach. Again, it is an argument that is entirely consistent with a communicative approach – but not necessarily the kind of quasi-communicative approach promoted by current coursebooks, where a sentence-level grammar still predominates.

Conversation is interactive, dialogic and communicative

It goes without saying that conversation is both interactive and dialogic. The value – even necessity – of interaction in language learning is generally accepted. Apart from anything, interaction provides opportunities for *output*, and without output there is less likelihood of *feedback*. The input-output-feedback loop is basic to cognitivist models of language learning.

Interaction is, of course, not the same as communication. Speakers can interact without necessarily registering what their co-speakers are saying. Communication implies more than this: it assumes the exchange and negotiation of meaningful messages. The capacity to do this – what's called *communicative competence* – is the goal of communicative language teaching. To this end, the communicative approach prioritises activities that require communicative interaction, such as *information gap* activities. In an 'info-gap', one learner has access to information that another learner does not, and vice versa. To achieve a satisfactory task outcome, they need to exchange the relevant information through talk.

However, the design of these activities often imposes a degree of artifice on the activity that is counterproductive. In an important critique of the communicative approach, Michael Swan characterised coursebook communication as being of the type: 'You are George – ask Mary what she does at Radio Rhubarb', and added: 'There are times when the same language practice can take place more interestingly and more directly if the students are simply asked to talk about themselves.' [7] It is a core tenet of the Dogme approach that when learners are communicating, communication should, first and foremost, be 'about themselves'. This is why conversation is promoted over mere communication, since conversation is the most common and the most appropriate vehicle for the exchange of interpersonal meanings.

Conversation scaffolds learning

The metaphor of conversation as a supportive, but temporary, *scaffold* for language development is central to the Dogme approach, and it is in this sense that conversation assumes its most important function. 'Scaffolding' is a term originally coined by Jerome Bruner to capture the way that the learning of any skill is co-constructed in the interaction between learner and teacher, whether the teacher is a parent, peer, sibling or actual teacher. The 'better other' provides the interactional support within which learners can feel safe enough to take risks and extend their present competence. The kind of conversational assistance that parents and siblings provide children as they develop conversational competence in their mother tongue is a classic instance of scaffolding at work. As the child becomes more fluent, the interactional scaffolding becomes redundant and is gradually 'dismantled'.

Because conversation is a natural context for verbal scaffolding, it has been argued that classroom talk that replicates the interactional features of natural conversation is likely to be more effective than traditional classroom talk, with its teacher-initiated question-answer routines. This is not to say that teaching should simply be free-ranging, informal chat. As Neil Mercer notes: 'Conversations in which people are self-consciously trying to teach and to learn will have special characteristics.' [9] To capture the nature of these characteristics, Roland Tharp and Ronald Gallimore coined the term 'instructional conversations':

The task of schooling can be seen as one of creating and supporting instructional conversations … . The concept itself contains a paradox: 'instruction' and 'conversation' appear contrary, the one implying authority and planning, the other equality and responsiveness. The task of teaching is to resolve this paradox. To most truly teach, one must converse; to truly converse is to teach. [10]

By seeking to embed learning opportunities within what Mercer calls the 'long conversation' of the lesson, Dogme is committed to resolving this paradox.

Conversation promotes socialisation

Conversation, in the real world at least, is not so much *transactional* as *interactional*. That is to say, when we chat with a friend, neighbour, or work colleague, it is not normally the exchange of information that is our main purpose. Rather, it is the establishing and maintaining of a 'good vibe': ie harmonious social relations. Even when our primary purpose might be transactional, as in a service encounter, or in the work place, we often book-end the transaction with small-talk, or what is known as 'phatic communication': communication whose purpose is solely or primarily social.

Phatic communication takes place in classrooms too, of course – typically at the beginning of the lesson, as learners arrive and the teacher organises the space, takes the register, and so on. Chatting has the beneficial effect of relaxing the group, and helping forge a group dynamic that is conducive to learning. But, traditionally at least, this interpersonal stage is not considered a part of the lesson. The lesson proper begins at a cue from the teacher – even at the expense of cutting the small-talk short, and thereby sacrificing some potentially valuable speaking opportunities, as in this extract from a classroom in Mexico. [12] (The numbers denote the length of a pause in seconds.)

> [After taking the register the teacher starts chatting to students.]
>
> **T:** well then, Jorge . . . did you have a good weekend?
>
> **S:** yes
>
> **T:** what did you do?
>
> **S:** I got married.
>
> **T:** [smiling] you got married. (0.7) you certainly had a good weekend then. (5.0) [laughter and buzz of conversation]
>
> **T:** now turn to page 56 in your books. (1.6) you remember last time we were talking about biographies . . . [T checks book and lesson plan while other students talk to Jorge in Spanish about his nuptials.]

Apart from the language practice opportunity that has been lost here, the teacher seems to be ignoring the important role that social processes play in language learning, and the way that conversation mediates these processes.

We saw earlier how Bruner's *scaffolding* metaphor foregrounds interaction and participation: in order to learn new skills, the learner participates in activity with a 'better other' and the new skills are jointly constructed. But learning involves participation in another, broader sense: *socialisation.* Here, participation is not only the co-construction of knowledge. It is also the process of becoming a member of what is called a 'discourse community'. This in turn means gaining acceptance as a legitimate speaker in that community.

'The language I learn in the classroom is a communal product derived through a jointly constructed process.'
Michael Breen [13]

From this perspective, L2 learning is not seen so much as a gradual and neutral process of internalising the rules, structures, and vocabulary of a standard language; rather, learners are seen to appropriate the utterances of others in particular historical and cultural practices, situated in particular communities. [14]

How this is achieved has been the subject of a growing number of studies aimed at charting the integration (or not) of individuals into particular discourse communities, and the role that language has played in the process. For example, Bonny Norton Peirce monitored the progress of a number of immigrant women in Canada over an extended period of time. She was able to account for their successes and failures to learn English by the extent that these women were socialised into particular discourse communities, and, specifically, the extent that these communities granted them the 'right to speak'. She writes that: 'An important implication of my study is that the second language teacher needs to help learners claim the right to speak outside the classroom. To this end, the lived experiences and social identities of language learners need to be incorporated into the formal second language curriculum.' [15]

'Teachers and learners are co-participants in the generation of classroom discourse.'
B. Kumaravadivelu [16]

An effective way of doing this is simply to make the classroom a discourse community in its own right, where each individual's identity is validated, and where learners can easily claim the right to speak. A conversational mode of classroom talk would seem to be better suited to establishing such a community than would a didactic one. Apart from anything else, conversation assumes a degree of equality between participants that blurs questions of status and social distance. This is another reason why a Dogme approach favours conversation: not just as the end, but as the means of language learning.

2 Materials-light

Since its inception, Dogme has had the reputation of being a movement whose goal it is, if not actually to *burn* coursebooks, at least to banish them from the classroom, along with any other materials and technological aids that teachers now take for granted. Dogme proponents have been labelled as luddites, iconoclasts, and ELT 'Amish folk'. This reputation is not entirely unfounded, of course.

Anti-texts?

The first article to appear under the Dogme banner called for the return to a pre-method 'state of grace' [17] – the classroom as simply a room with a few chairs, a blackboard, a teacher and some learners, and where learning is jointly constructed out of the talk that evolves in that simplest, and most prototypical of situations. As an instance of a stripped-down, minimally-resourced style of teaching, the example of the visionary New Zealand educationalist Sylvia Ashton-Warner was invoked. She narrates an incident where she consigns all her materials and texts to the school incinerator. 'You should have heard the roaring in the chimney!' [19]

But it is worth emphasising at this point that a Dogme approach is not anti-materials nor anti-technology *per se*. What it rejects are those kinds of materials and aids that don't conform with the kinds of principles outlined earlier. Materials that might just conform to these principles would be those that support the establishment of a local discourse community, and which foster the joint construction of knowledge, mainly through mediated talk.

Unfortunately, ELT materials do not, generally speaking, support these ends. For a start, the sheer amount of published material available threatens to stifle the opportunities for conversation that (as we have argued) are so important for language development. By reducing the amount of material that is imported into the classroom, the teacher frees the learning space for the kind of interactive, talk-mediated learning opportunities that are so crucial for language development. As Ashton-Warner observed, after her moment at the incinerator, 'teaching is so much simpler and clearer as a result. There's much more time for conversation … communication.' [21]

Pretexts

Of course, materials *could* provide a stimulus for real communication and conversation, and many textbook writers include discussion and personalisation tasks to this end. But, more often than not, these good intentions are subverted by the not-so-hidden agenda of most ELT materials: to teach grammar – or rather, to promote the delivery and consumption of 'grammar McNuggets', ie pre-selected, pre-graded, (pre-digested?) grammatical items such as the present continuous or the past perfect, irrespective of any perceived need, relevance, or utility. Helen Basturkman, for example, analysed the back cover blurbs of a range of current coursebooks. Based on the high frequency of mentions of words like *grammar*, *vocabulary* and *language*, she concluded that 'the ELT community views language as a core of grammatical structures and vocabulary' and that 'the emphasis [is] on the underlying generative base or language rules rather than on surface level aspects of use' [22]. Grammar rules, and for many teachers, it's difficult to justify putting time aside for small-talk when there are grammar structures to teach and to test. Thus, grammar tends to fill the time available for teaching it.

Even the texts that are included in standard textbooks are less texts than *pre*texts [24] for the reinforcement of the grammar syllabus and are rarely tapped for their communicative potential. Their capacity to engage the learner cognitively or affectively is a secondary concern, hence their banality. As Karen Grady puts it: 'The textbook represents all types of issues and all types of discourse as not requiring much thought or action beyond the decision as to the appropriate grammatical structure – everything is reducible to form.' [25]

Subtexts

More suspect, perhaps, than their pretexts, coursebooks also have *sub*texts. That is, they embed cultural and educational values that may have little to do with the needs of the learner, especially the learner of English as an *International* Language (EIL). They may even serve to 'undermine the alternative styles of thinking, learning, and interacting preferred by local communities'. [26] Over twenty-five years ago, Gillian Brown noted that coursebooks promoted a kind of English that she called 'cosmopolitan English' because 'it assumes a materialistic set of values in which international travel, not being bored, positively being entertained, having leisure, and above all, spending money casually and without consideration of the sum involved in the pursuit of these ends, are the norm' [27]. Claire Kramsch attributes the materialism of coursebook content partly to the utilitarian objectives of the communicative approach, which 'brought language use down to the functional level of streets and supermarkets, under the emulation of the authentic white middle-class native speaker.' [28] And yet the consumerist nature of coursebook content also reflects the aspirations of many learners of English, who view the acquisition of English (rightly or wrongly) as a passport to material well-being and international travel.

Depending on your own ideological position, you may be happy to support learners in achieving these goals. On the other hand, you may feel that the learners' aspirations are being manipulated in the interests of globalisation and/or the hegemony of English, and that coursebooks simply serve these wider interests. As B. Kumaravadivelu notes:

Because of the global spread of English, ELT has become a global industry with high economic stakes, and textbook production has become one of the engines that drives the industry. It is hardly surprising that the world market is flooded with textbooks not grounded in [the] local sociocultural milieu. [30]

Teachers, like it or not, are complicit in these globalising processes. As Alistair Pennycook points out, 'English language teaching beliefs, practices and materials are never neutral. … It might be said that the English language class may be less about the spread of English than about the spread of certain forms of culture and knowledge.' [31] Pennycook identifies these forms of culture and knowledge as being essentially Western, capitalist, and neo-colonialist. The most concrete embodiment of these forms of culture and knowledge is, of course, the coursebook.

Contexts

One way of resisting the covert values that coursebooks embody is by critiquing – or 'interrogating' – them. Kumaravadivelu, for example, recommends 'asking learners to discuss how topics could be dealt with differently, from the point of view of their own linguistic and cultural perspective'. [32] A second approach is to 'go local', and use only locally produced materials (if they are available). Or, at the very least, produce versions of coursebooks tailored for specific contexts. John Gray, who interviewed a number of teachers about their attitudes to coursebooks, concludes that 'it is certainly the case that the teachers I spoke to about global materials clearly felt the need for what might be called a "glocal" [ie a global-plus-local] coursebook – something which could give them "a better fit" and simultaneously connect the world of their students with the world of English'. [33]

A third approach might be to abandon teaching materials altogether. This is in fact what happened, inadvertently, to John Wade, a volunteer teacher in the 1960s. Wade describes how he was recruited to start up, alone, an Australian government primary school deep in the rainforests of New Guinea. Having lost the few materials he had in an accident (his pack-horse fell into a flooded ravine), he describes how, impelled by the children's needs and interests, he covered the primary school curriculum by working from what was immediately available. 'I asked the children to show me what they wanted to know about, and gradually introduced English through their responses. … We did our math and science in the bush by estimating how many kernels we could get from an ear of corn. We checked with the villagers where and how far apart we should plant them, and how big an area we would need to clear …', and so on [35]. Out of this experience, Wade evolved a textbook-free pedagogy that, he maintains, 'not only empowers your learners, it also makes the teacher's job in the classroom a lot more fun and much easier'. [36]

Own texts

The critique of language textbooks, on the grounds of their atomistic approach to syllabusing and their aspirational cultural content, is part of a wider, anti-positivist, post-

'In teaching English we can impart to learners not only the present perfect, but also the power of knowing and caring about the world they live in.'
Luke Prodromou [29]

'The total meaning of a language course for any one student is the net effect it has on him (or her).'
Earl Stevick [34]

colonialist discourse that has its roots in what is known as 'critical pedagogy'. *Positivism* is the belief that knowledge exists, independently of the learner, as a body of facts that can (and should) be transmitted from teacher (and textbook) to learner. The Brazilian reformer Paulo Freire, a pioneer of critical pedagogy, argued that, from the positivist perspective education is viewed as an 'act of depositing':

… in which the students are the depositories and the teacher is the depositor. […] This is the 'banking' concept of education, in which the scope of action allowed to the students extends only as far as receiving, filing and storing the deposits … In the banking concept of education, knowledge is a gift bestowed by those who consider themselves knowledgeable upon those they consider to know nothing. [37]

As an alternative to this 'banking' model of education, Freire advocated a 'dialogic' pedagogy, in which the learners become not simply the objects of the teaching process, but agents in their own education:

Through dialogue, the teacher-of-the-students and the students-of-the-teacher cease to exist and a new term emerges: teacher-student with student-teachers. The teacher is no longer merely the-one-who-teaches, but one who is himself taught in dialogue with the students, who in turn while being taught also teach. [39]

To achieve this objective, Freire proposed that the educational process should be grounded in the local needs and concerns of the participants. 'Whoever enters into dialogue does so with someone about something; and that something ought to constitute the new content of our proposed education.' [40] This meant basing learning on themes that were elicited in consultation with the learners themselves, and replacing the imported texts with the learners' own texts. In the same spirit, Sylvia Ashton-Warner replaced primary school readers (that had been imported from a white, middle-class British context) with homegrown materials that the (mostly Maori) children generated out of their own raw experience. Around the same time, but independently, two educationalists in the USA, Neil Postman and Charles Weingartner, called – provocatively – for a five-year moratorium on the use of all textbooks:

Since with two or three exceptions all text[book]s are not only boring but based on the assumption that knowledge exists prior to, independent of, and altogether outside of the learner, they are either worthless or harmful. If it is impossible to function without textbooks, provide every student with a notebook filled with blank pages, and have him [sic] compose his own text. [41]

Whole texts

An alternative to a positivist, discrete-item, grammar McNugget view of language learning is the more holistic approach offered by what is called 'whole language learning'. The whole language movement is largely a North American phenomenon, although it has parallels with other 'deep-end' approaches, such as task-based learning and project work, which may be more familiar in European circles. The major tenet underlying whole language learning is that:

… language is best learned in authentic, meaningful situations, ones in which language is not separated into parts, ones in which language remains whole. Whole language integrates reading, writing, listening and speaking and defines the role of the teacher as one of facilitator and the role of the student as an active participant in a community of learners. [42]

The basic principles for a whole language approach have been spelt out by Yvonne and David Freeman [43]:

- Learning goes from whole to part.
- Lessons should be learner-centred because learning is the active construction of knowledge.
- Lessons should have meaning and purpose for learners now.
- Learning takes place in social interaction.
- Reading, writing, speaking and listening all develop together.
- Lessons should support learners' first languages and cultures.
- Faith in the learner expands learning potential.

'Liberating education consists of acts of cognition, not transferrals of information.'
Paulo Freire [38]

'A curriculum that promotes only segmented, isolated, and elemental learning tasks reduces the students' degree of learning (including incidental learning) and also their preparedness for future learning.'
Stuart McNaughton [44]

These principles – it should be obvious – are very 'Dogme' in both wording and spirit. The similarities do not end there. A whole language learning approach – because it is anti-positivist – is also sceptical about the value of textbooks. Here is a statement of its position on materials:

Expensive elaborate materials are not needed when implementing whole language approaches. Students read texts that are familiar and meaningful, drawing on familiar concepts and experiences to which they can relate. It is not necessary to purchase elaborate 'units' designed by publishing companies, material that often controls the curriculum by failing to consider student need and input. The whole language teacher does not worry about a pre-ordained sequence or hierarchy of skills; the curriculum becomes organised as teacher and students share planning. [45]

Other texts

Where do the learners get the 'texts', that are so familiar and meaningful, you may be wondering. More or less anywhere, of course. One thing that there is no shortage of in this digital era is texts – and texts in English. In fact, the enormous availability and accessibility of texts – both written and spoken – is one very good reason why, as teachers, we need be less dependent on textbooks than, say, in the 1970s and 1980s. As an example of how the internet can support the development of homegrown course materials, Olga Kulchytska describes how an advanced class of hers in Ukraine designed and wrote what they called their 'Alternate Textbook'. They chose their own themes and texts. 'All the creative work would be theirs, and I would just be the administrator,' she writes. 'Something amazing happened when I said, "Don't pick topics for teachers – you are going to write this textbook for yourselves and for the next few generations of students." My inert students started naming issues I had never suspected they were interested in.' [46] These are the themes they collectively chose:

> 1. The Individual and Society
>   a. Alcoholism, Smoking, Drug Abuse
>   b. AIDS
> 2. People's Values
> 3. Human Rights
> 4. The World after World War II
> 5. Careers
> 6. Man and Nature
> 7. Youth Culture
> 8. Women and Society
> 9. The Art of Love

'Students themselves are in a unique position to look for relevant resource materials. They know what their own needs and interests are.'
David R. Hall [47]

Commenting on the experience, one of the students said: 'Working on the Alternate Textbook gives us the opportunity to choose themes which are more important and useful than those in the textbook. Besides, it makes us read a lot of authentic texts.' [48] Not only does the Alternate Textbook conform with the principles of whole language learning, its local and learner-driven nature makes it perfectly compatible with a Dogme approach.

Learning texts

Inspired by what she had read of the Dogme approach, Nerina Conte, a teacher of an elementary children's class in Barcelona, describes an initiative in which the children produced their own portfolios of work, complete with sketches and photos. She justifies this approach on the grounds that children don't need books to learn a language when they can draw on their own background and experiences. Moreover, 'when students come and ask for a course, they come to learn English, they don't come to do a book. They want the book as a back-up. I've never heard a student say, "I want to do such-and-such a book."' [49] When asked if her planning time was increased by not having a coursebook to work from, Nerina was emphatic: 'No, not at all. One way of saving time is by personalising, by speaking about your own life, bringing in pictures. I started off this year speaking about my pet. 'My dog's name is Nikita', etc. And later, when I showed them just a list of words that they'd copied from the blackboard, they said "This is about Nikita". And it was. They immediately knew what it was about, so it's really powerful.'

In an article that pre-dates Dogme by several years, Dick Allwright challenged the hegemony of coursebooks, at least in their traditional role as 'teaching materials'. His point was that what we now need are 'learning materials' and he alluded to a 'general change in the conception of teacher and learner responsibilities for the management of language learning'. [51] How would this power shift impact on published materials? Allwright suggests that 'something much less ambitious, probably locally produced, would seem preferable'. The preceding accounts of different 'alternative textbooks' would seem to meet these criteria. So too did the Dogme injunction to adopt a 'materials-light' approach:

Materials-mediated teaching is the 'scenic' route to learning, but the direct route is located in the interactivity between teachers and learners, and between the learners themselves. [52]

🖪 Focus on emergent language

Critics of a Dogme approach are quick to seize on its apparent lack of structure or methodological rigour. How can it qualify as sound practice if so much seems to be left to chance? Even teachers who are predisposed to a Dogme-type approach (maybe because they feel constrained by the current coursebook-driven orthodoxy) are often nervous about the consequences for their learners. 'How can I ensure that they *learn* anything?' and 'Will I cover the syllabus?' are questions that go to the heart of their concerns.

Uncovering versus covering
To counter these concerns, proponents of a Dogme approach argue that learning – and language learning in particular – is an *emergent* process, and that it is less to do with *covering* items on a syllabus than *uncovering* the 'syllabus within'. That is, if learners are supplied with optimal conditions for language use, and are motivated to take advantage of these opportunities, their inherent learning capacities will be activated, and language – rather than being *acquired* – will *emerge*.

Such a belief seems to have resulted from John Wade's experience in the highlands of New Guinea in the 1960s. If you remember, Wade lost all his teaching aids and so developed an approach that simply used the resources of the real world around him. What is particularly interesting about this experience is that, when he finally saw a copy of the primary school syllabus, he was gratified to find that he had covered just about every item listed. 'So I put the syllabus away and continued as I had been doing.' [54]

It might be more accurate to say that Wade had – not covered – but *un*covered the curriculum. That is, through the kinds of tasks and projects he set up, he had provided the means by which the learners' language needs could be satisfied naturally and organically. The notion of 'teaching to the learners', rather than 'teaching to the curriculum', is one that is shared by both the Dogme approach and whole language learning. As Strickland and Strickland put it: 'Whole language teachers use materials that suit the needs of the class, and the curriculum is, to a great extent, the product of interaction between the teacher and the students.' [55]

Communication versus code
The principle of choosing and using materials 'that suit the needs of the class' is fundamental to the design of *English for Special Purposes* (ESP) courses, where the learners' needs are identified in advance and programmes are designed accordingly. It is also a principle of *English as a Second Language* courses, eg courses that prepare immigrants to integrate into a predominantly English-speaking society. And, of course, the idea that instruction should meet the curricular needs of learners is a basic to *content teaching* (also

'I harness the communication since I can't control it, and base my method on it.'
Sylvia Ashton-Warner [50]

'Language learning emerges from participation in linguistic practices, such practices always being steeped in historical, cultural and institutional meaning systems.'
Leo van Lier [53]

'The class is not a class in the traditional sense, but a meeting-place where knowledge is sought and not where it is transmitted.'
Paulo Freire [56]

known as 'Content and Language Integrated Learning' or CLIL). Learners of general English, however, are assumed to have no identifiable needs, and so, by default, are taught random items of grammar and vocabulary (ie the code), with no clear communicative aim in sight. And this is going on when most teachers would claim to subscribe to a *communicative approach.*

If you remember, the communicative approach developed out of the concept of *communicative competence* – the notion that there is more (maybe a lot more) to proficiency in a language than knowing the linguistic systems involved. If you make communication your aim, you need to think in terms of teaching more than simply grammar and vocabulary. One of the early proponents of Communicative Language Teaching, Dick Allwright, argued that 'a logical extension of the argument would suggest that if communication is *the* aim, then it should be *the* major element in the process.' [57] Allwright went on to reason that *any* attempt to control the selection and sequencing of syllabus items 'would be most likely to interfere with learning, since, given the state of our knowledge in such matters, it could only be appropriate by chance'. [59] Instead, he advocated an approach whose basic tenet is that the best way to learn how to communicate is by communicating. As he put it:

If the 'language teacher's' management activities are directed exclusively at involving the learners in solving communication problems in the target language, then language learning will take care of itself ... [60]

Hence, early proponents of a communicative approach argued for a syllabus of tasks rather than of discrete language items. The basic premise of a task-based approach is, in Dave Willis's terms, 'that out of fluency comes accuracy, and that learning is prompted and refined by the need to communicate'. [61] Where a Dogme approach parts company with a task-based approach is not in the philosophy but in the methodology. As we have argued, naturally-occurring talk is a sufficiently fertile context for language development, obviating the need for the somewhat artificial and cumbersome tasks associated with a task-based approach.

A commitment to the belief that 'learning will take care of itself' found an echo, in the USA, in the work of Stephen Krashen. Like Allwright, Krashen also argued against the need for formal instruction, and on the same grounds: that it may unnecessarily inhibit natural processes of acquisition. But, for Krashen, what triggers these processes is not interaction, but input. In his words: 'Speech cannot be taught directly but "emerges" on its own as a result of building competence via comprehensible input.' [63] Accordingly, methodologies were designed (such as 'Total Physical Response') that rejected explicit teaching of grammar, and instead provided learners with masses of comprehensible input. The success of immersion programmes in bilingual contexts such as Canada added supportive evidence to Krashen's claims for the value of input, and for the need for a 'silent period' before productive skills kick in.

Process versus product

These 'deep-end', non-interventionist, theories found a receptive audience in the 1970s and 1980s, where the buzz-word was *learner-centredness*. The notion of the learner-centred curriculum found a natural ally in the communicative approach. Faith in the ability of syllabuses – and of teaching generally – to deliver knowledge 'on a plate' was replaced by a faith in the potential of collaborative tasks to provide the right conditions for learning to occur. As David Nunan sums it up:

Proponents of learner-centred curricula are less interested in learners acquiring the totality of the language than in assisting them gain the communicative and linguistic skills they need to carry out real-world tasks. [64]

Put another way, the learner-centred curriculum was less concerned with the products of learning (in the sense of knowledge of grammar, lexis, or functional exponents) than in the processes of communicating and learning. This process orientation reached its logical conclusion in the notion of the 'process syllabus'. A process syllabus is a syllabus that grows organically out of the needs and interests of the learners: there are no pre-selected goals or specifications of content. It is also a *negotiated* syllabus. That is, the content of the syllabus, and even the methodology itself, is subject to a continual process of negotiation and evaluation by learners and teacher.

The ongoing consultation with learners that is built into the process syllabus recognises that, not just ESP or ESL learners, but EFL learners too, have needs and interests that can – and should – shape the content and objectives of their language course. These needs may not be as concrete, as utilitarian, nor as stable as, say, those of a banker or an aid worker, who need English for their professional activities. The language needs of general English learners will evolve and ramify as their language competence increases, and as their discourse community coalesces. It is not for the teacher (nor the absentee coursebook writer) to second-guess these needs: the learners should be involved in articulating these from the outset.

In a process approach (and in a Dogme one, therefore) it is not the coursebook grammar that structures the teaching programme. Instead, it is the *learner's grammar.* As Dave Willis argues:

In helping learners manage their insights into the target language we should be conscious that our starting point is the learner's grammar of the language. It is the learner who has to make sense of the insights derived from input, and learners can only do this by considering new evidence about the language in the light of their current model of the language. This argues against presenting them with pre-packaged structures and implies that they should be encouraged to process text for themselves so as to reach conclusions which make sense in terms of their own systems. [66]

The idea of the process syllabus has been influential at a theoretical level, but has been rarely put into practice in a systematic and deliberate way. The lack of uptake may be due, in part, to the domination of the coursebook: a coursebook is virtually incompatible with a negotiated syllabus. In many ways, though, a Dogme approach rehabilitates the principles and practices of a process syllabus. By doing away with the coursebook, and hence dispensing with the pre-selected list of grammar items that form the coursebook's backbone, a Dogme classroom devolves a degree of agency to the learners in terms of determining both the content and the objectives of their language learning experience. Like a process approach, a Dogme approach does not assume that general English learners have no needs, nor does it attempt to plug this supposed gap with a diet consisting of nothing but grammar McNuggets.

Emergence versus acquisition

Basic to such approaches as the process syllabus, task-based learning, whole language learning, and, of course, Dogme, is the belief that – given the right conditions – language emerges. But what does it mean to say that language emerges? We can think of language emergence as operating at two levels. On the one hand, language emerges out of interpersonal classroom activity. Given a good dynamic and sufficient incentive, learners engage collaboratively in the production of language output. That is one reason for foregrounding conversation. On the other hand, as the learners engage in these classroom processes, their internal language system (or *interlanguage*) responds and develops in mysterious ways: learners produce language that they weren't necessarily taught, and sometimes show unexpected quantum leaps in their development. In this intrapersonal sense, language also emerges.

Our understanding of the way language emerges, both interpersonally and intrapersonally, has benefited from developments in the study of complex systems in nature. Emergence – the idea that certain systems are more than the sum of their parts, and that 'a small number of rules or laws can generate systems of surprising complexity' [69] – is a relatively new development in science. It has been enlisted to explain how birds flock or how an ant colony is capable of reacting in unison to a threat. Because there is no 'central executive'

'Process in teaching and learning is principally a matter of the quality of communication between teacher and students and, especially, between students.'
Herbert Puchta and
Michael Schratz [67]

'Out of the slimy mud of words ... There spring[s] the perfect order of speech.'
T. S. Eliot [68]

determining the emergent organisation of these systems, the patterns and regularities that result have been characterised as 'order for free'.

Some scholars – notably Diane Larsen-Freeman, Lynn Cameron and Nick Ellis – have been studying language through the lens of complexity theory, both in the way languages develop in society, and in the way that a learner's first language (or the second language learner's *interlanguage*) develops over time. They believe that language development displays many of the characteristics of an emergent system. As Diane Larsen-Freeman puts it: 'Language is not fixed, but is rather a dynamic system. Language evolves and changes … [it] grows and organises itself from the bottom up in an organic way, as do other complex systems.' [71]

The processes by which language 'grows and organises itself' are relatively simple. They are processes that are basic to human cognition and hence not specific only to language. As Nick Ellis explains: 'Language is cut of the same cloth as other cognitive processes.' [72] These processes include the capacity to extract patterns from input, the capacity to form and strengthen associations, and the capacity to chunk sets of already formed associations into larger units. By means of these simple operations, acting upon massive input, sound and word sequences are chunked into larger units, out of which emerges the complexity we call grammar.

Similar conclusions have been reached by linguists working in the field of corpus linguistics. Michael Hoey, for example, has looked at the evidence of large data-bases of naturally occurring language (*corpora*) and noted how particular words and word-combinations (*chunks*) recur in the same patterns. Hoey argues that, through repeated use and association, words are primed to occur in predictable combinations and contexts. He concludes that 'what we think of as grammar is the product of the accumulation of all the lexical primings of an individual's lifetime'. [74]

It seems that a theory of language and a theory of learning have found common ground, both suggesting that language is an emergent phenomenon, driven by massive exposure and use.

Second language versus first language

Given enough exposure and use, then, it would seem that language emergence – at least, *first* language emergence – is the inevitable result. So, why is this not the case in second language learning? Sadly, the processes that make first language acquisition so easy, such as chunking and pattern extraction, function far less successfully for second language acquisition. Why is this?

For a start, the intricate associative network that has been created for the first language tends to inhibit the forming of new associations in a second one. Also, the ability to discriminate sounds in a second language is much less sensitive than in the first, where the system was primed at infancy, when the neural 'stuff' was at its most plastic. Because so many grammatical distinctions – such as verb endings, auxiliaries, articles and prepositions – are phonologically reduced in naturally occurring talk, it is often difficult to pick them out. To compensate, the learner tends to rely, not on grammatical markers, but on words, both in interpreting speech and in producing it. Through repeated use, this simplified system may become entrenched, especially when it seems to 'do the job', communicatively speaking. Finally and importantly, the much reduced input and practice opportunities available to most learners mean that – for a system whose emergence depends primarily on usage – progress, if any, will be slow.

Responsive teaching versus pre-emptive teaching

Even advocates of usage-based acquisition admit that the process can be speeded up by some kind of direct intervention. What form should this intervention take? Nick Ellis suggests that acquisition can be facilitated 'by making the underlying patterns more salient as a result of explicit instruction or consciousness-raising'. [75] That is to say, if learners are having trouble identifying and abstracting patterns, their attention can be purposefully directed at them.

This is what some writers, including Michael Long, have termed a 'focus on form'. A focus on form 'overtly draws students' attention to linguistic elements as they arise incidentally in lessons whose overriding focus is on meaning or communication'. [76]

Note that Long is not advocating the explicit teaching of grammar items in advance of communication, but as the need arises during communication. This is an approach that is entirely consistent with the Dogme view – that the grammar syllabus (and also the lexical one, for that matter) should emerge, not as an attempt to anticipate the learners' communicative needs, but *in response* to them. That is, it is a syllabus that is both usage-driven and responsive.

A focus on form, then, aims to redress the weaknesses in the second language learner's innate capacity to notice, tally and abstract patterns from the input and re-use these abstracted patterns as output. This requires of the teacher much more than simply providing the conditions for language emergence. The language that emerges must be worked upon. It must be scrutinised, manipulated, personalised and practised. There are many ways that the teacher can encourage learners to engage with emergent language so that it does not simply remain dormant and inert. Below is a list of ten strategies that may be considered crucial:

1. **Reward** emergent language. Show learners that you value their output. This does not mean excessive praise, but simply some sign that learner participation and creativity is welcome in your class.
2. **Retrieve** it. Otherwise it will just remain as linguistic 'noise'. This might mean simply making an informal note during a speaking activity, or, at times, writing a learner's utterance on the board.
3. **Repeat** it. Repeat it yourself; have other learners repeat it – even drill it! Drilling something has the effect of making it stand out from all the other things that happen in a language lesson.
4. **Recast** it. Reformulate the learners' interlanguage productions into a more target-like form. This is not the same as correction. It is simply a way of indicating 'I know what you're trying to say; this is how I would say it'.
5. **Report** it. Ask learners to report what they said and heard in groupwork. Apart from anything else, knowing that they may have to report on their groupwork encourages learners to pay attention to what is going on.
6. **Recycle** it. Encourage learners to use the emergent items in new contexts. This may be simply asking for an example of their own that contextualises a new item of vocabulary, or it may involve learners creating a dialogue that embeds several of the new expressions that have come up.
7. **Record** it. Make sure learners have a written record of the new items. Writing something down not only helps fix it in memory, but it's a good way of conferring importance on material that has come up incidentally.
8. **Research** it. Help your learners to find regularities and patterns in the emergent language. This may involve asking them to formulate explicit rules, or simply to find some kind of pattern or regularity in a number of items.
9. **Reference** it. Link emergent language to the 'external' syllabus objectives. This helps satisfy the need of some learners to know that the emergent syllabus bears some relation to the formal syllabus, as it is represented in the coursebook, for example.
10. **Review** it. At the end of the lesson, ask your learners to write five words they have learned. Have them share what they have learned. Do this again at the beginning of the next lesson. All learning, after all, is simply remembering that you have understood something.

None of this is rocket science! These are techniques that relatively inexperienced teachers can apply, using minimal resources. The secret lies in being confident in the knowledge that these simple procedures are *all* that is required to ensure successful – and enjoyable – language learning.

Another way of teaching

Dogme, as we have seen, takes as axiomatic three principles, all of which have antecedents in other educational traditions, and all of which imply the use of specific practices and strategies in the classroom. It may be worth restating that these are not prescriptions, about what teachers *should* do. Nor are they proscriptions, about what they *shouldn't* do. (Dogme rejects dogma!) Rather, they represent the distillation of a set of practices reported by a growing number of teachers around the world, who are committed to a Dogme approach:

Because Dogme is about teaching that is ***conversation-driven***, this implies:

- establishing a classroom dynamic that is conducive to interactive talk;
- setting up conversations between and about 'the people in the room';
- taking advantage of conversation as it occurs incidentally;
- providing the necessary scaffolding to support talk in a second language;
- being a participant oneself in the classroom talk.

Because Dogme is about teaching that is ***materials-light***, this means:

- orienting lessons to the learners' needs and interests;
- foregrounding the learners' topics and texts;
- making the most of minimal means;
- if using materials, using ones that are locally generated;
- challenging the assumptions inherent in imported materials.

Because Dogme is about teaching that is ***focused on emergent language***, this means:

- setting up activities that are language productive;
- using learner language to inform lesson and course planning;
- viewing learners' errors as learning opportunities;
- retrieving instances of learner language and analysing them;
- recording, reviewing and recycling instances of learner language.

Another way of being a teacher

In proposing an alternative to transmission-type, teacher-led teaching, Claire Kramsch wrote:

A dialogic pedagogy is unlike traditional pedagogy … it sets new goals for teachers – poetic, psychological, political goals that … do not constitute any easy-to-follow method. … Such a pedagogy should better be described, not as a blueprint for how to teach foreign languages, but as another way of being a language teacher. [78]

Dogme, too, is more than simply a new set of techniques and procedures. It is more an attitude shift, a state of mind, a different way of *being* a teacher. In fact, because it prioritises the local over the global, and the particular over the general, the individual over the crowd, a Dogme approach will vary according to its context. For some teachers and in some situations, it may be enough to intersperse their teaching with 'Dogme moments', such as when a learner's utterance offers a learning opportunity and the lesson takes a brief detour in pursuit of it. Other teachers may be motivated to – or in a position where they are allowed to – design their whole course according to Dogme principles.

Dogme techniques and activities don't in themselves constitute a fixed 'method' or a 'one-size-fits-all' prescription for effective teaching. We hope, though, that by experimenting with these techniques and activities in ways that are sensitive to your teaching context, you start to experience another way of being a language teacher.

Bibliography

1 Allwright, R L (1984) 'The importance of interaction in classroom language learning' *Applied Linguistics*, 5

2 McArthur, T (1992) *Concise Oxford Companion to the English Language* OUP

3 Wittgenstein, L (1967) *Philosophical Investigations* OUP

4 Hatch, E (1978) 'Discourse analysis and second language acquisition' In Hatch, E (Ed) *Second Language Acquisition: A book of readings* Rowley, M A Newbury House

5 Lewis, M (1993) *The Lexical Approach* LTP

6 Kress, G (1985) *Linguistic Processes in Sociolinguistic Practice* Deakin University Press

7 Swan, M (1990) 'A critical look at the communicative approach' In Rossner, R and Bolitho, R (Eds) *Currents of Change in English Language Teaching* OUP

8 Cadorath, J and Harris, S (1998) 'Unplanned classroom language and teacher training' *ELT Journal*, 52 (3)

9 Mercer, N (1995) *The Guided Construction of Knowledge: Talk amongst teachers and learners* Multilingual Matters

10 Tharp, R G and Gallimore, R (1988) *Rousing Minds to Life: Teaching, learning and schooling in social context* CUP

11 van Lier, L (1996) *Interaction in the Language Classroom* Longman

12 Cadorath, J and Harris, S op. cit.

13 Breen, M (1985) 'The social context for language learning – a neglected situation?' *Studies in Second Language Acquisition*, 7

14 Norton, B and Toohey, K (2001) 'Changing perspectives on good language learners' *TESOL Quarterly*, 35 (2)

15 Peirce, B N (1995) 'Social identity, investment, and language learning' *TESOL Quarterly*, 29

16 Kumaravadivelu, B (1993) 'Maximising learning potential in the communicative classroom' *ELT Journal*, 47

17 Thornbury, S (2000) 'A dogma for EFL' *IATEFL Issues*,153 (2)

18 Gates, W *The Times*, 8th October, 1997

19 Ashton-Warner, S (1963, 1980) *Teacher* Virago

20 Postman, N (2000) *Building a Bridge to the Eighteenth Century: How the past can improve our future* Random House

21 Ashton-Warner, S op. cit.

22 Basturkman, H (1999) 'A content analysis of ELT textbook blurbs: reflections on theory-in-use' *RELC Journal*, 30 (1)

23 de Montaigne, M (1575) *Essays*

24 Pulverness, A (1999) 'Context or pretext? Cultural content and the coursebook' *Folio*, 5 (2)

25 Grady, K (1997) 'Critically reading an ESL text' *TESOL Journal*, 6 (4)

26 Canagarajah, A S (1999) *Resisting Linguistic Imperialism in English Teaching* OUP

27 Brown, G (1990) 'Cultural values: the interpretation of discourse' *ELT Journal*, 44 (1)

28 Kramsch, C (2005) 'Post 9/11: Foreign languages between knowledge and power' *Applied Linguistics*, 26 (4)

29 Prodromou, L (1992) 'What culture? Which culture? Cross-cultural factors in language learning' *ELT Journal*, 46 (1)

30 Kumaravadivelu, B (2003) *Beyond Methods: Macrostrategies for language teaching* Yale University Press

31 Pennycook, A (1994) *The Cultural Politics of English as an International Language* Longman

32 Kumaravadivelu, B op. cit.

33 Gray, J (2002) 'The global coursebook in English Language Teaching' In Block, D and Cameron, D (Eds) *Globalization and Language Teaching* Routledge

34 Stevick, E (1980) *Teaching Languages: A way and ways* Heinle & Heinle

35 Wade, J (1992) *Teaching without Textbooks* CIS Educational

36 ibid.

37 Freire, P (1970, 1993) *Pedagogy of the Oppressed* Penguin

38 ibid.

39 ibid.

40 Freire, P (1973) *Education for Critical Consciousness* Continuum

41 Postman, N and Weingartner, C (1969) *Teaching as a Subversive Activity* Penguin

42 Strickland, K and Strickland, J (1993) *Un-covering the Curriculum: Whole language in secondary and postsecondary classrooms* Boynton/Cook Publishers

43 Freeman, Y and Freeman, D (1998) *ESL/EFL Teaching: Principles for success* Heinemann

44 McNaughton, S (2002) *Meeting of Minds* Learning Media

45 Strickland, K and Strickland, J op. cit.

46 Kulchytska, O (2000) 'The Alternate Textbook' *The Journal of the Imagination in Language Learning and Teaching*, Vol 5: http://www.njcu.edu/CILL/vol5/kulchytska.html

47 Hall, D R (2001) 'Materials production: theory and practice' In Hall, D R and Hewings, A (Eds) *Innovation in Language Teaching: A reader* Routledge

48 Kulchytska, O op. cit.

49 Conte, N and Thornbury, S (2003) 'Materials-free teaching' *English Teaching Professional*, 26

50 Ashton-Warner, S op. cit.

51 Allwright, R (1981, 1990) 'What do we want teaching materials for?' In Rossner, R and Bolitho, R (Eds) *Currents of Change in English Language Teaching* OUP

52 Thornbury, S (2005) 'Dogme: Dancing in the dark?' *Folio*, 9 (2)

53 van Lier, L (2004) *The Ecology and Semiotics of Language Learning: A sociocultural perspective* Kluwer

54 Wade, J op. cit.

55 Strickland, K and Strickland, J op. cit.

56 Freire, P (1970, 1993) *Pedagogy of the Oppressed* Penguin

57 Allwright, R (1979) 'Language learning through communication practice' In Brumfit, C and Johnson, K (Eds) *The Communicative Approach to Language Teaching* OUP

58 Legutke, M and Thomas, H (1991) *Process and Experience in the Language Classroom* Longman

59 Allwright, R op. cit.

60 Allwright, R op. cit.

61 Willis, D (1990) *The Lexical Syllabus: A new approach to language teaching* Collins ELT

62 Newmark, L (1966) 'How not to interfere with language learning' Reprinted in Brumfit, C and Johnson, K (Eds) (1979) *The Communicative Approach to Language Teaching* OUP

63 Krashen, S (1985) *The Input Hypothesis: Issues and implications* Longman

64 Nunan, D (1988) *The Learner-centred Curriculum* CUP

65 Larsen-Freeman, D (2002) 'Language acquisition and language use from a chaos/complexity theory perspective' In Kramsch, C (Ed) *Language Acquisition and Language Socialization* Continuum

66 Willis, D (1994) 'A lexical approach' In Bygate, M, Tonkyn, A and Williams, E (Eds) *Grammar and the Language Teacher* Prentice Hall

67 Puchta, H and Schratz M (1993) *Teaching Teenagers* Longman

68 Eliot, T S (1974) *Collected Poems 1909–1962* Faber

69 Holland, J (1998, 2000) *Emergence: From chaos to order* OUP

70 Lewin, R (1993) *Complexity: Life on the edge of chaos* Phoenix

71 Larsen-Freeman, D (2006) 'The emergence of complexity, fluency, and accuracy in the oral and written production of five Chinese learners of English' *Applied Linguistics*, 27 (4)

72 Ellis, N (2001) 'Memory for language' In Robinson, P (Ed) *Cognition and Second Language Instruction* CUP

73 Ellis, N (1997) 'Vocabulary acquisition: word structure, collocation, word-class' In Schmitt, N and McCarthy, M (Eds) *Vocabulary: Description, acquisition and pedagogy* CUP

74 Hoey, M (2005) *Lexical Priming* Routledge

75 Ellis, N (1997) op. cit.

76 Long, M (1991) quoted in Doughty, C and Williams, J (Eds) (1998) *Focus on Form in Classroom Second Language Acquisition* CUP

77 Ellis, R (1994) *The Study of Second Language Acquisition* OUP

78 Kramsch, C (1993) *Context and Culture in Language Teaching* OUP

B

Teaching Unplugged is a process of exploration. Since our first experiences as trainee teachers, we build up a stock of teaching strategies and task types, ranging from things we may take for granted, such as being friendly or writing information on the board during a lesson, to new ideas. Exploring a new teaching approach like Dogme involves reassessing our stock of strategies and task types, *adapting* some whilst *adopting* others.

The teaching strategies in the following pages are particularly well suited to the unplugged classroom. Many are tried and tested favourites, used by the authors over the years; others have been written specially. All are presented as activities that you can try out in class with a minimum of preparation.

Unplugged activities

We have used a consistent structure for the activities which will quickly start to feel familiar: there are suggestions for things to consider and to do *before*, *during* and *after* the lesson.

Other elements which may be familiar to teachers are absent. There are no language

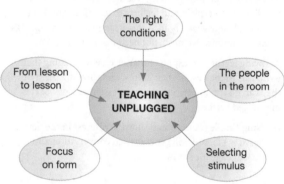

exponents (the language will emerge from the activity), no timings (this will depend on where your class take the activity), and no levels (these activities are designed to adapt to and reflect the abilities of the learners). There are no worksheets to photocopy: each activity is ready – with perhaps a little homework from yourself and your learners – to use. They are designed to come to life in class.

The activities do not need to be tried in order – the five chapters here are interrelated. As you experiment, you will find that some suit your teaching context perfectly, and that others work much better with a tweak here and there. Make the changes yourself – highlight or delete on the printed page; note down your own ideas in the margins. The activities are yours to unplug.

Unplugged teaching

Learning a language is also a process of exploration. There are false starts and wrong turns along the way and, in fact, progress as a learner is impossible without them. Teaching, although we may feel exposed at times, is the same. Enjoy yourselves – both you and your learners!

Creating the right conditions

Traditionally, learners come to class to be 'given' a lesson that has been prepared in advance by the teacher.

In the Dogme classroom, it's the other way round: learners bring the lesson with them – in the 'rough form' of their language and lives – and the teacher helps them to shape it into a learning experience.

An unplugged teacher can do this anywhere in the world, without published materials or even (if necessary) electricity, but it isn't a magical process. Unplugged teaching is rooted in reality, because the essential resources are already there in the room.

The ingredients for teaching are present the moment you and the learners get together, and this chapter will show you how to use four key resources to create the right conditions for unplugged learning, right from the start.

Learners

The learners are your primary resource. They have stories to tell, ideas to explain and feelings to describe. This isn't just what language is 'about' – this *is* language. Form springs from communicative need, not need from form.

Allowing learners to express themselves, encouraging them to do this to the best of their ability, and showing them how they can do it more effectively, is the essential work of the unplugged teacher.

By using simple prompts and showing interest in the detail of everyday life, you will generate rich conversation and ample language for study.

Language

Of course, the learners aren't there just to tell their stories. They are there because they want to improve their English, or because someone else thinks it would be a good idea for them to do so.

How people come to be studying English – and what they see themselves doing with it – is one of the basic things teachers need to understand.

Asking how the people in your class feel about English, and finding out about how the language fits into their lives, will help you to understand their expectations and level of motivation.

Paper

You will need more than pen and paper to teach unplugged, but not much more. If a stick in the sand would enable you to perform the basic functions of noting and adjusting learner language, a whiteboard and markers will prove much more convenient! The presence of a whiteboard and markers (or blackboard and chalk) in the classroom is taken for granted in *Teaching Unplugged*, although access to an interactive whiteboard is not.

It's not that technology should be avoided on principle: there are activities in *Teaching Unplugged* featuring the internet and mobile phones. It is more that it should be used actively. Using *basic* resources allows you and your learners to be hands-on with language, and using paper in all shapes and sizes (small Post-it® notes can be invaluable) in the learning process – from noting and drafting to passing round the room – is fundamental.

Place

It is easy to forget how much stimulus there is around us. There is space, to make our own. There is sound, inside and outside the room. There's the world, seen and heard through a window. Colleagues interrupting your class can provide ready-made listening practice that has immediate relevance to learners' lives.

Unplugged teaching doesn't focus exclusively on the minutiae of the school environment, but it does seek to maximise the potential for generating conversation and the language of what is immediate, live and real.

Creating the right conditions

Tips and techniques

1 Trying Dogme isn't an 'all or nothing' moment. You can keep using your coursebook as you experiment with these activities, building up the amount of 'unplugged' teaching you do as you go along. So experiment in small ways to start with, and take time to get used to the flow of language and activity in the Dogme classroom.

2 Explain what you are doing. If your class are used to using published materials all the time, tell them that you are trying something different. Highlight what you have achieved together at the end of the lesson, together with anything you expect to do in the next one: this will show people that the lessons are not without structure, and that the learners are getting at least as much value as they might from a more conventional approach.

3 Always be sensitive to the mood in the room. See the activities you initiate as *suggestions* rather than *instructions*: explain them clearly and encourage everyone to do their best, but be realistic and good-humoured if an activity isn't really working. You can always bring it to a close.

4 Open up the classroom space. If you can, arrange chairs or desks in a circle, so that everyone can make eye-contact with everyone else at all times.

5 Vary your own position in the room. Rather than using a teacher's desk, try sitting with the learners, using a free seat in the circle or moving your own seat around the room. Standing up can help when you are explaining how an activity is going to work. Walking to the board to make notes will change the focus. Moving around will give you energy, and this will be infectious.

6 Give learners the chance to vary their position in the room, too. Use different combinations of pairs and groups. Invite people to work alone at their seats or to mingle on their feet. Where appropriate, invite them to use the space adjacent to the classroom for groupwork: stairs, yards and empty rooms can all be used in this way.

7 Using examples from the learners' own usage for your teaching is highly motivating. You don't have to constantly correct: get into the habit of making discreet notes as people speak, capturing examples of successful usage as well as words and phrases that are causing problems, especially if they come up more than once in conversation. This will give you the 'raw material' you need for a focus on form later in the lesson.

8 See *everything* as a language opportunity. For example, if you run your finger over a surface and find it is dusty, share the moment with the learners: ask them what you are reacting to, ask them how they feel about it, elicit and extend the words they have for talking about it.

9 The activities in *Teaching Unplugged* aren't designed to generate specific exponents, but you can ask yourself what language areas are *likely* to be generated. Revise these in advance if it helps you to feel more confident – but be prepared for all the other language that will emerge!

10 Teaching unplugged should be fun – for all concerned. Everyone in class is there to be welcomed, each activity is there to be enjoyed. Before it is a language lesson, an unplugged lesson is a social event. The language flows from there.

The right conditions mean your language learners are relaxed and ready to talk. Key terms:

- **Encourage** – always be positive, and generous with praise.
- **Explain** – tell people what *you* are doing, and why you want *them* to do it.
- **Help** – the activities are not tests, so suggest ways to get started and keep going.

Show that you are focusing on *their* language:

- **Highlight** – point out the things you would like them to notice.
- **Adjust** – make small changes as you repeat or write up their language.
- **Extend** – help them to build on their existing language.

How I got my name

Sharing the stories behind people's names

Think about it
Everything is a potential starter for conversation, from everyday events to basic information such as our names.

Get it ready
There's nothing to prepare.

Set it up
Write everyone's first name on the board, then write the following questions:
> Does your name have a meaning?
> Does anyone else in your family have that name?
> Is it a popular name in your country/region?

Tell the students to move around and ask each other the questions. Tell them they can ask you the questions, too.

Let it run
- Everyone mingles and asks the questions on the board to at least three people.
- You join in, helping with language and generally encouraging, as appropriate.
- When they have finished, each person tells the whole class about how a classmate got their name, until the story behind everyone's name has been told.

Round it off
As a class, discuss the most common – and the more unusual – reasons for being given a name. As you talk, note on the board any words or phrases you would like to focus on later.

Broaden the discussion by asking questions like these:
> What is the most unusual name you have heard of in your country/region?
> Is it good to be given a very unusual name?

Discuss the words and phrases you have noted on the board. Explain, adjust and answer questions, as required.

Follow-up
For homework, or in the next lesson, everyone writes a short text about 'How I got my name', using some of the words and phrases that were highlighted and practised.

Always, sometimes, never

Sharing everyday likes and dislikes

Think about it
People usually enjoy talking about themselves and this can generate plenty of relevant language. Using a simple framework can help to get the conversation started.

Get it ready
Make a note of three things concerning yourself: one which you *always* enjoy, one which you *sometimes* enjoy, and one which you *never* enjoy (see the authors' examples below).

Set it up
Divide the board into three columns and label them: *I always enjoy*, *I sometimes enjoy* and *I never enjoy*.

Tell the class about the three things *you* have noted, without saying which is which. When they have guessed, and you have talked about it together, write each in the correct column on the board.

Let it run
- Everyone notes down three activities, one for each column, without indicating to anyone else where they belong.
- People share their answers in pairs; their partner guesses which activity belongs in each column and they discuss the 'correct' answers.
- You circulate, make notes, help with language and generally encourage, as appropriate.

Round it off
When they have finished, invite everyone in turn to come to the board and write the activities of their partner in the appropriate column. Discuss these as you go along.

Use your notes to highlight form, explaining, adjusting and extending.

Follow-up
Working individually for homework or in groups in the next lesson, the class write a report on the things that are most and least popular. You can suggest phrases that will be useful in this report, such as:
> Lots of people enjoy …
> Only a few people enjoy …

Authors' examples

	Always	Sometimes	Never
Luke	Cooking	Washing up	Cleaning the oven
Scott	Browsing in second-hand bookshops	Shopping for food	Shopping for clothes

Same time, different day

Talking about life outside school

Think about it

Sharing information about our lives helps to build the class dynamic, making it easier to generate everyday conversation from lesson to lesson.

Get it ready

There's nothing to prepare.

Set it up

Tell the class to imagine that it is exactly the same time, but on a different day: they are doing whatever they normally do when they aren't in class. (It can be a weekend day, or another day of the week when you don't meet as a class.)

Hand out slips of paper.

Let it run

- Everyone writes down what they 'are doing' on their slip of paper, without showing it to anyone. You collect the papers, mix them up and read one out. For example: *Someone's working in a café … picking up their children from school … playing computer games … ,* etc.

- The class guess who it is, and ask the person who wrote it some questions about what they normally do. This is repeated until everyone has talked about themselves.

- As they talk, you make notes, help with language and generally encourage, as appropriate.

Round it off

Ask the class to work in groups to complete phrases like these:

> *Most people …*   *A few people …*
> *Some people …*   *One person …*

Tell them to dictate their sentences to you; you write them on the board as they do this, without adjusting the language.

Ask the class if there are any improvements that can be made to the sentences on the board.

Make any changes they suggest, and explain any additional ones of your own: these may relate to accuracy, or to range of expression.

Variation

Ask the class the same question, but use a different scenario. Here are some possible examples:

> *It's the weekend*   *It's ten years in the future*
> *It's ten years ago*   *It's 200 years ago*

These alternative time frames can be used with past and future tenses, too, but we often revert to the present tense once a hypothetical scenario (past or future) has been established. For example: 'Ten years in the future? I'm probably playing with my children.'

Best in 24

Describing something we really enjoyed

Think about it

A reliable conversation starter draws on experiences that we have every day. Food and drink are obvious subjects and are a good way for people to start getting to know each other in more detail.

Get it ready

Bring some dice to class.

Set it up

Give everyone in the room, including yourself, a number. Roll the dice and ask the person corresponding to the number that comes up:

> *What's the nicest thing you ate or drank in the last 24 hours?*

Ask them a few more questions yourself. For example:

> *What was so good about it?*
> *Where did you eat it? Who with?*
> *Where did you buy it? How did you cook it?*

When you have had a brief conversation, elicit these additional questions from the learners and write them on the board, adjusting as required.

Let it run

- The student who answered your questions throws the dice, and 'passes on' the initial question (*What's the nicest thing … ?*) to the person indicated – you help them to reconstruct this question, if necessary.

- The conversation continues as a whole-class activity, in open pairs. In larger classes, the students can work in groups.

- You listen, help with language and generally encourage, as appropriate. As you listen, write down on Post-it® notes any words or phrases that you would like to discuss with the class – one word or phrase per note.

Round it off

Put your language notes up on the walls. Invite everyone to go round, read them and mark a maximum of three words or phrases they would like to explore.

Focus on the one with the most 'votes', then the next, etc.

Discuss these words and phrases with the class in the order they have chosen, adjusting, explaining or extending as required.

Variation

Some alternative conversation starters:

> *What made you laugh (or smile)?*
> *Most enjoyable conversation?*
> *Most interesting TV programme/website/ newspaper article/photo?*
> *Cheapest/Most expensive purchase?*

My English

Telling the story of why we're studying

Think about it

It's good to share your own experience of learning a language. Talking about this, including the things you found difficult, will help to give your class the confidence to discuss their own experiences.

Get it ready

Think about a language you have learned (to whatever level), and consider the phrases below.

Set it up

Tell the class when you started learning a second or other language – this can be English. Tell them when you use it now, and what helps you to improve.

Dictate the following phrases:

> I started learning English …
> I use English now (when/where) …
> It helps when …

Let it run

- Working individually, the class complete the phrases in writing.

- They then share their answers in pairs.

- You monitor, make notes, help with language, and generally encourage as appropriate.

Round it off

Divide the board into three, using the three sentence starters as headings. Invite people to come to the board and write the phrases their partner used to complete each sentence.

Get feedback from the class on what has been written on the board. Is there anything that could be improved? Adjust as appropriate, using the feedback and your own suggestions, and answering any questions that arise.

Discuss the notes under It helps when … , and encourage people to share their tips for improving their English.

Follow-up

For homework, people find someone to interview about how they use their English, and report back to the class. These interviews could be conducted with friends, family members or other acquaintances – they could also be conducted by e-mail.

Variation

Ask people to find out about someone's experience of learning any second or other language – it doesn't have to be English, as people will still be sharing their experience of language learning.

This street, this town

Thinking about how people are using English

Think about it

People's reasons for learning English can be varied and not always entirely clear. Thinking about the ways in which *other* people are using English outside the classroom can help people to imagine how *they* can use it themselves.

Get it ready

You need the board to be clear for this activity. The circles you draw needn't be perfect, but they do need to be BIG.

Set it up

Draw three large concentric circles on the board. Label the centre one *This street*, the middle one *This town*, and the outer one *This country* (see the diagram below).

Let it run

- In pairs or small groups, the class draw their own copies of the target diagram you drew on the board.

- They discuss the following questions and fill in their diagrams:

> Who do you think is using English right now in each circle?
> Is English their first language?
> Are they reading, speaking, writing, listening?
> Who are they communicating with, and about what?

- When they have finished, they compare their conclusions with another group or pair.

- You circulate, make notes, help with language and generally encourage, as appropriate.

Round it off

Invite each pair or small group to come to the board and write up their suggestions, explaining them to the class.

Ask the class where they see *themselves* in that picture, now or in the future. Where can they imagine using English, and for what reasons?

Follow-up

Encourage people to take any opportunities that are open to them to practise their English. Ask them whether they have actually been able to do this, and to share their experiences with the class.

Party, what party?

Exploring confidence and motivation

Think about it
The way we feel about speaking another language is often linked to feeling confident – but it's also connected with a willingness to experiment.

Get ready
There's nothing to prepare.

Set it up
Tell people to imagine they have been invited to a party – and it's one they really want to go to!

Ask them to imagine what their party is like, and to make individual notes of the following:
Where will it be held?
What sort of people will be there?
What sort of atmosphere will there be?

Let it run
- In pairs, people tell one another about their imaginary parties. After a time, you elicit and write on the board the different types of party they have imagined. For example: sleepover, house party, dinner party, etc.
- Tell them that while their parties will be the same in every other way, they must now consider something else: the language(s) that people will be speaking there. Still working in pairs, they must now choose between:

Party 1: Everyone speaks their native language only (ie everyone speaks the same language).

Party 2: Everyone speaks English only.

Party 3: People speak a mix of languages, including English and their first language.

- Working in small groups (two or more pairs per group) they discuss which party they would most like to go to. You circulate, make notes, help with language and generally encourage.

Round it off
In whole class, find out which is the most popular party in each group. Explore the reasons behind their choices, and discuss the benefits of practising and experimenting with English.

Using your notes, highlight some relevant language that has emerged: explain, adjust and extend, as appropriate.

Follow-up
Everyone writes an account of the party they chose, using some of the language that has been highlighted above.

Everyone's a teacher

Learning from each other

Think about it
Inviting your class to teach *you* from time to time is fun for everyone – and will give people an insight into the challenges of teaching and learning in general, and language in particular.

Get it ready
There's nothing to prepare.

Set it up
Choose some phrases that have emerged in the course of a week's lessons and which you would like to be able to say in another language. If you and your learners all speak the same language, have a look at the Variation below.

Let it run
- Write your selection of phrases on the board, and check for understanding by asking different people to explain the meaning of each phrase to the rest of the class. Say that you want them to teach you how to say them in their language.

  In a *multi-lingual class*, everyone chooses a phrase and translates it into their language, ready to teach you.

  In a *monolingual class*, people work in groups and each group agrees on three phrases to teach you.

Round it off
Each person, or each group, teaches you their phrases. You can ask for help with your pronunciation, although you probably won't need to ask – people will be happy to volunteer advice!

Variation
You can invite people to teach you a fact of some sort, instead – the important thing is to give them a chance to do some teaching! It can be anything at all, provided you don't already know it: something connected with a personal hobby or interest, for example anything from aircraft to computer games. People can work in groups to pool their ideas and choose a number of facts to teach you. They can even test your memory at the end of the week.

Paper whispers

Passing on messages on small pieces of paper

Think about it

When we need to write something down, we often have to do it in a hurry. Noting things quickly in class for other people to read can help to make writing an everyday classroom activity.

Get it ready

Write a number of short messages – around 15-20 words – on slips of paper. For example:

> *Something you did at the weekend*
> *An announcement to do with school*
> *A short recipe*
> *Directions to a local shop*

Arrange the seating so that everyone is in a line or circle.

Set it up

Pass the first message to someone in the class: they have a short time to read it (15-30 seconds, depending on the message) without showing it to anyone else, after which they hand it back to you.

Invite them to write the same message, as accurately as they can, on another slip of paper.

They then pass their note to the next person, who reads it and hands it to you before writing their own version of the note. This is repeated until everyone has written their version of the message and the last version has reached the end of the line or completed the circle.

Read out the final version, and compare it with the original.

Let it run

- The activity is repeated, but with two different messages passing in the same direction at once. You can get one of them started at the beginning of the line and the other one half-way down (or on the other side of the circle), so the ones at the end don't have to wait too long.
- Collect the messages as you go, keeping them in order.
- Compare the final version of each with the original.

Round it off

Stick the notes that you have collected up on the board, in order. Invite everyone to stand up and look at the sequences. What changes have occurred during the process? Look at the ways in which words and phrases have been affected, and explore the differences.

Follow-up

Use messages written by the class this time: everyone writes a sentence of their own and shows it to you for comment and suggestions, before making a final draft on a slip of paper. The activity is repeated, using some of their messages.

Graffiti

Taking notes on large pieces of paper

Think about it

Asking people to do something unexpected can be motivating in itself, and in this activity people get to write on the walls – well, almost.

Get it ready

Fix some large sheets of blank paper to the walls around the room (one for each group you will form). If possible, ask the class to help you to do it at the start of the lesson.

Set it up

Tell the class that the walls are now the whiteboard, and that they are going to use this space to make some notes from their conversations.

Divide the class into groups, each positioned near one of the sheets of paper. You sit with one group (away from the whiteboard).

Set up an activity like *Best in 24* (see page 27), for example, by asking someone in the class what they most enjoyed eating or drinking over the past 24 hours.

As this person speaks, write on the nearest sheet of paper on the wall two key items of information: what they were eating, and why they enjoyed it.

Let it run

- In their groups, the class continue this process, with one person asking the question and writing up notes on their 'personal whiteboard' and the next person answering, and so on, until everyone has spoken.
- You circulate, encourage and help with language as they do this, making notes on a sheet of your own, based on words or phrases that you helped with.
- Each group removes their sheet of paper from the wall and works together to make sentences from the notes. For example, they fill out the note *kimchi – favourite* with: *Cho enjoyed having kimchi for lunch. It's one of her favourite foods and it reminds her of home.*

Round it off

When they have finished, ask each group to pass their sheet on to the next group. Invite each group to study the sheet they have been given, and to ask the group who handed it to them any questions they may have.

Finally, use the notes on your own sheet to feed back on language used by the class and any adjustments that they can make.

Variation

An alternative is to use whiteboards on easels around the class. People can also write on Post-it® notes instead of sheets of paper, and stick these to the walls.

Disappearing text

Using pen and paper instead of photocopies

Think about it

Handing out photocopies can save time, but it is a very passive way for students to experience a text. It can be much more engaging to use basic copying techniques, combined with a memory challenge.

Get it ready

Choose a short text. Using a marker pen and a large sheet of paper, make a copy large enough for the whole class to read.

Set it up

Tell the class you will be putting a text up on the board for them to see, and that they need to copy it down as accurately as possible. But they will only be able to see it for one minute!

Display the text for one minute, then take it down.

Let it run

- The class have another minute to check their work.

- They turn their copies over. You tell them you will be putting the text up again, this time for thirty seconds only, and that this will be their last chance to check their copy for accuracy. After thirty seconds, take it down.

- From memory, they make any changes they want to make to their own work, before comparing versions with a partner.

Round it off

Ask one pair to dictate to you what they think is an accurate copy. Write it up on the board, then display the original text and discuss any differences with the class, or any language issues that arise.

Follow-up

As another memory challenge, people try in pairs or small groups to remember the text in as much detail as possible – without referring to their notes.

Variation

Working with the class, build a dialogue using a situation that has come up in class (for example in a text, or in the learners' lives). Write the dialogue on the board, and organise the class into pairs.

Each taking a part, the first pair read the dialogue out.

Before the next pair read it, each person in the first pair erases two or more words (they choose which words, but you work out the number of words to erase, based on the length of the text and the size of the class).

Continue pair by pair, until the dialogue has disappeared completely, and the pairs are 'reading' from memory.

Paper interviews

Writing questions and answers

Think about it

Asking people to write questions, rather than ask them verbally, creates an interesting dynamic in class, with opportunities for a focus on form during the activity.

Get it ready

Prepare some slips of blank paper. If you can, make a number of sets in different colours.

Set it up

Set the scene by reporting a recent event in your life, such as *Last month I went abroad* or *On Sunday I went to a party.*

Tell the class that they are going to write a short report of that event, so they need to ask you questions. But instead of *speaking*, they are going to ask the questions *in writing*.

Organise the class into three or four groups. Distribute a dozen or so slips of paper to each group. (It helps if each group has different coloured paper.)

Let it run

- Each group decides on a question they want to ask, in order to get information that will be useful for their report. They write the question on one of the slips of paper and one member of the group 'delivers' the question to you. If the question is correctly formed (and relevant), you write the answer on the same slip of paper.

- The 'postman' then returns to the group where the answer is read and a new question formulated and delivered to you for answering. If a question is not well formed, you send it back, perhaps with some indication as to where it needs adjusting.

- When each group has assembled sufficient information, they can then start to use this information to write an account of the event (which should be in the third person). During this stage, the groups are allowed to 'post' you more questions if they find that they are lacking important information.

- When the accounts have been written, each group passes their text to the group on their right. The texts are read, and then passed on to the next group. Because the questions that each group asked will be different, each group's text will also be different.

Round it off

Discuss these differences in whole class. For example, ask individuals to mention any differences they found between their account and those of other groups.

Variation

Use events from the learners' lives as stimulus, with their classmates using written questions to interview them before writing their accounts.

Space travellers

Using the whole classroom

Think about it

Moving around the room and making the most of all the available space is good for people's energy levels: movement also dramatises debate around simple statements.

Get it ready

Prepare a number of statements that might provoke a range of opinion. They don't need to be statements you believe, just ones that you think will get people talking. For example:

I like Mondays.   *Homework is a waste of time.*
TV is bad for you.   *Britney Spears is wonderful.*
Cheese is delicious.

Write the following phrases, each on a large sheet of paper: *Agree, Disagree* and *Not sure.*

Set it up

Place the *Agree* sheet at one end of the room, the *Disagree* sheet at the other, and *Not sure* in between the two, in the middle of the room.

Tell people that these represent three 'positions' they can take, depending on how they feel about a statement you are going to write on the board.

Write one of your statements on the board.

Let it run

- Each person stands up and moves to the appropriate part of the room. They then tell the two people nearest them why they have chosen that place to stand.

- On your invitation, people start to explain the position they have chosen to the whole class. Don't challenge the reasons they give, but do ask them to tell you more, helping with language as appropriate.

- While this is happening, you note on the board examples of the language that you help with – including words that caused problems and any phrases that you added to the conversation.

Round it off

Invite people to move if they heard anything they found persuasive, and to tell the class why they are moving.

Discuss the language on the board, and check meaning.

Add a twist to your initial statement. In the examples above, you could substitute *Friday* for *Monday, the internet* for *TV*, and so on. Invite people to move again, and ask those who have moved why they have done so.

Follow-up

Using some of the words that you have written on the board, everyone writes down their opinion of the original statement, and then of the 'twisted' statement.

The sounds of silence

Using your surroundings as stimulus

Think about it

You don't need to reach for published materials to generate vocabulary. Language is all around us, waiting to be tapped.

Get it ready

Open the windows. If your classroom doesn't have windows, open the door.

Set it up

Tell the class:

Be very quiet for one minute. Don't speak, just listen to the sounds inside and outside the classroom.

Silence, with a smile, anyone who speaks.

Give everyone a Post-it® note, and explain that you want them all to write down something about what they can hear – a description of the sounds, or even a response to them: what the sounds make them think or feel. You can write some example phrases on the board:

I can hear some birds singing.
The sound of birds makes me think of the countryside.

Let it run

- Everyone writes down something about what they can hear: a description of the sounds, a response to them, what they think, what they feel. They put their note up on the wall.

- People walk around the room and read what everyone else has written. They choose their favourite note, apart from their own, and stand next to it.

- When everyone is ready, they tell the class why they like the note they have chosen.

Round it off

Starting with the words that people have written down, and adding words of your own, list on the board as many words as possible to describe what can be heard, inside and outside the room.

Think of everything, from ticking watches (or beeping mobiles) to the hum of the neon light.

Explain, refine and extend the language that has emerged, as appropriate.

Follow-up

Working individually, people imagine they are somewhere very different – and write down what they can 'hear' there. They show you their first draft, and make any improvements you suggest. They read out their second draft to the class: everyone else has to guess the place they are describing.

Variation

Instead of writing, the class draw what they hear.

Every sight, every sound

Making the best of a distraction

Think about it

If you are flexible and show interest in something your class have been distracted by, you can create a learning opportunity.

Get ready

All sorts of things can create a distraction in class, from a wasp entering the room to a loud noise outside. Let's imagine, for example, that there is a loud thunderstorm.

Set it up

Taking your cue from the class reaction, invite them to talk about it.

Ask how people feel about it, and discuss the reasons behind their feelings. Supply any words they are reaching for.

Let it run

- Working in small groups, people think of as many positives and negatives about the thunderstorm as they can.

- You monitor, make notes, help with language and generally encourage, as appropriate.

- While people are still talking, you divide the board into two columns. Label one *Good* and the other *Bad*.

Round it off

Invite someone from each group to write their positives and negatives on the board. Are there more of one than the other? What do *you* think about it? Add one or two of your own.

Finally, ask the same groups to decide on the five words or phrases that are most useful for talking about a thunderstorm, and then compare their selections.

Follow-up

Everyone writes an account of the thunderstorm, from one of the following points of view:

> Their own, as someone in class at the time
> Someone who was outside at the time

Or, more poetically:

> The point of view of the storm
> The point of view of the streets or fields

Outside in

Making the most of an interruption

Think about it

Most language use takes place in busy environments. Opening the classroom to visitors and interruptions can help to create a more spontaneous atmosphere, which is closer to the way we process language outside class.

Get it ready

Encourage colleagues to come into class if they ever need to make an announcement about school life, from course details to parties and lost property. It doesn't have to be a very important announcement, provided it is relevant and 'true to life'.

Set it up

Welcome your colleague, listen to what they have to say and invite your class to ask them questions about it.

Let it run

- Once the visitor has left, the class work in pairs to reconstruct, in writing and as accurately as possible, what your colleague said on coming into the room.

- As they do this, you make your own reconstruction.

- In small groups, people compare their own text with other people's, before agreeing on a composite version.

Round it off

Ask one of the groups to dictate this version back to you and write it on one half of the board, keeping the other half clear. Ask other groups what they think: answer any questions and make any corrections they suggest.

Now write your own version on the board for comparison, discussing any differences (even small ones).

Follow-up

Working in groups, the class change the 'spoken' text into a 'written' announcement, making any necessary adjustments to the sort of language used. For example: What is the shortest text that will convey the message in question?

Managing conversation

At its simplest, a Dogme lesson involves talking about life, and then talking about the language this has generated. Life and language are intimately linked: the language we use to talk about them is relevant to our needs as learners.

'Talking about life' is not quite as simple as it sounds. It demands a constant, active participation from the teacher that balances the benefit of 'letting things run' with the need to maintain pace and focus. With time and experience, this can start to feel like an organic process, but in truth there are many strategies we adopt to sustain, develop and, effectively, manage conversation.

We do this by being alive to the ways in which it develops naturally: by prompting and participating; by encouraging everyone to make full contributions; and by 'nudging' the conversation in different directions, to ensure challenge and variety from day to day. And more than anything, we do it by showing interest in the lives of the people in the room.

Me, you, and what we do

Coursebooks usually try hard to be interesting: big topics, important issues, glamorous faces. Lessons shouldn't be boring – far from it – but directing learners' attention to what is big, important and glamorous can mean that a lot of interesting detail gets missed.

Much of what we discuss with family, friends, partners and colleagues is the stuff of everyday life: the things we enjoy doing, the things we have to do, the things that go wrong and the things that go right. Sometimes this arises spontaneously and can be shaped into a learning opportunity; at other times, setting a simple task can help to get the ball rolling.

Feelings and things

The way learners feel on a given day has traditionally been seen as incidental to what happens in class. Of course, it's important to keep going and focus on the lesson; people don't come to school just to 'have a moan'. But that doesn't mean we shouldn't talk about the mood we're in, good or bad. After all, the way we feel affects more than our receptiveness to learning opportunities – it shapes our communicative needs, often giving us a reason to speak in the first place.

By engaging with the way people feel, we allow learners to express themselves more fully, and help to build the class dynamic.

Sharing, comparing

As soon as you have more than one person in a room (and this includes the teacher!), you have a chance to compare experiences and opinions. This is especially true when, as in many adult classes and increasingly in general, learners come from a range of nationalities and backgrounds.

Survey-style activities can be motivating for learners of all ages. They are a great way to get people on their feet and interacting with each other, whether they are talking about everyday habits, personal preferences or more intangible things such as memories.

Dreams and schemes

Focusing on the lives of the people in the room naturally includes our hopes and fears, which are as much a part of everyday life as a trip to the shops. The tasks in this section are likely to promise to 'nudge' learner language into areas such as modality and conditionality, but this may not happen: not only can these forms arise in *any* context, they may *not* arise when you expect them to. We often talk about learner language as if it waits upon form, but in reality it is brought to life – and shaped in unexpected ways – by context. We need to keep an open mind about the language that will emerge!

Managing conversation

Tips and techniques

1 Think of your class as people first, and as language learners second. Show interest in them and their lives. If you allow this to drive your teaching, the language they need as learners will follow.

2 Pay attention to what people are saying and not just the language they are using. If you focus too much on form, you will miss what is being communicated – and people will notice.

3 Always remember that *you* are one of the people in the room! You can set the tone for class conversation by sharing real experiences from your everyday life – though nothing too personal. No one should feel they have to talk about anything they don't want to.

4 Always use people's names during conversation activities, and encourage your class to do the same when they address or refer to each other. If you need to, prompt with a smile and the question: *Name?* At the beginning of a course, and if the people coming to your class vary from week to week or even lesson to lesson, it can help to write everyone's name on the board at the start of each lesson.

5 Be friendly and alert, and be sensitive to how people are feeling. Everyone gets in a bad mood sometimes, but if someone looks really down then do try and speak to them. You can take them aside at a break, or ask if you can have a word after the lesson. You may not be able to help personally if something is amiss, but you might be able to suggest someone who can.

6 Start small: relish the detail in everyday life, and build conversation from there. Asking the right questions can help to nudge the conversation into new directions, and this will encourage people to extend their language use.

7 Open (*wh-*) questions generate richer answers than closed (*yes/no*) questions. A question such as: *What was the best bit of your weekend?* is likely to be more productive than: *Did you have a good weekend?*

8 Teaching unplugged is designed to *uncover* language, rather than to *cover* specific language items. Engage with people and what they are saying, rather than worry about where the activity is going in terms of language output. But this in no way prevents you from refining the language that emerges, as is demonstrated in more detail in the chapter where the 'focus is on form'.

9 Keep your eyes and ears open for potential stimulus. If people come into the room laughing or talking animatedly about something, don't be afraid of showing interest. Ask them what's funny, and respond to the content of what they say. Allow time for this exchange, and bring others into the conversation as well.

10 Playing background music is often helpful. It can create a relaxed or stimulating atmosphere when people arrive, and a little ambient noise will encourage people to keep going when there are natural pauses in the conversation. Playing background music a little louder will stop pairs and groups from overhearing each other's conversations when they are working on outputs which they are to share later in the lesson. Whatever music you choose, be sure to vary it, and to use your learners' own recommendations as appropriate.

Managing conversation means being actively involved, especially at first. Key terms:

- **Participate** – take part in conversation as a person, not just as a teacher.
- **Engage** – show genuine interest in the people in the room, and in what they say.
- **Model** – show how conversations can begin, by demonstrating with a learner.

Step back as conversation starts to flow, but:

- **Prompt** – by inviting people to say more, and inviting everyone to participate.
- **Comment** – by pausing the conversation to highlight something that is proving difficult.
- **Nudge** – by guiding the conversation into areas that will challenge the class.

All about us

Answering questions about ourselves

Think about it

Most of us enjoy talking about ourselves, and this activity is good for building confidence.

Get it ready

Have some dice ready.

Set it up

Explain that everyone has suddenly become very famous, and that they will each be holding a 'press conference' where they answer questions from the class about their daily lives.

Suggest areas the class can ask about. For example: *food, people, places, work, relaxation.*

Give everyone in class a number, and roll dice to decide who goes first.

Let it run

- People take it in turns to be interviewed – to make it more like a real press conference, you can set a time limit.

- You use occasional prompts to encourage longer answers. For example:
  Tell us more …
  Oh, really? Why was that?

- As the conversation develops, you note down on a piece of paper examples of usage – both effective and less effective – and of any words or phrases that you find yourself helping people with.

Round it off

Write on the board some of the words or phrases you have noted.

Explain, adjust and answer questions. Suggest ways of extending the language that has emerged, as appropriate.

Tell people to work in pairs, and to remind each other of what was revealed in their 'press conference', incorporating the new language.

Follow-up

Everyone writes five sentences, each of which should include one of the words or phrases on the board.

Variation

You can use the same activity with people choosing to actually 'be' a celebrity. The rest of the class must guess who they are.

Something we did

Chatting about recent events in our lives

Think about it

Talking about everyday life generates language that is immediately relevant to the participants. Often this will happen spontaneously, but a simple task framework can help, especially if learners are unused to being invited to chat in this informal way.

Get it ready

There's nothing to prepare.

Set it up

Write on the board the following phrases:
Something you did with someone else
Something you did that you don't usually do
Something you didn't manage to do

Tell the class they must choose a sentence from the board that describes something they did or didn't do since the last lesson.

Ask one student to tell you which sentence they have chosen, and ask them some questions about it. Invite them to ask you in the same way.

Elicit from the class some of the question types that have been used and write these on the board, adjusting as necessary, as examples for use in the next phase.

Let it run

- Working in pairs, the class tell each other about what they did.

- You circulate, answering questions, helping with language and generally encouraging. Where there is little interaction between partners, you prompt them to ask for more information, asking example questions yourself.

- The class exchange partners, which gives them a chance to repeat the exercise following your input.

Round it off

Brainstorm some of the words and phrases that have emerged in conversation. Adjust the forms as needed, answering any questions, before suggesting ways of extending the language.

Follow-up

Elicit the opposite of the original phrases, for example: *Something you did on your own.*

Everyone writes a sentence about something else they did since the last lesson, using one of the opposites as a prompt.

Give feedback on these, ask people to redraft and then read out their new versions.

Jorge's wedding

Sustaining conversation started by learners

Think about it

We plan activities to 'get people talking' – but if they're already talking, so much the better! (This activity is named in honour of the learner mentioned in Part A of *Teaching Unplugged*, who got married but didn't get to talk about it.)

Get it ready

If a conversation has started before the lesson or in the break, whether in English or in another language, be prepared to follow it up.

Set it up

Show that you're interested, using facial expression as much as words.

If people are happy to keep talking, involve the other people in the room (as they arrive or come back after the break, for example). Comments can be as effective as actual questions in encouraging participation: *Jorge got married at the weekend!*

Then ask Jorge if he is happy to keep talking about his wedding. If he is, divide the class into pairs. If not, don't worry – let it go with a smile.

Let it run

- Each pair thinks of a question for Jorge. They show you a draft; if a pair shows you a question you have already seen, ask them to think of another question.

- Each pair in turn asks Jorge their question.

- Listening to their questions and Jorge's answers, you quietly note words and phrases on the board, adjusting as necessary, without putting them in any order.

Round it off

The conversation will naturally generate a number of lexical sets, one of which will be the vocabulary of getting married: *bride*, *groom*, and so on. But other lexical sets will emerge (sometimes unexpectedly) from the real-life account. These might include *stress*, *parties*, *expense*, etc.

Identify for the class two or three headings for lexical sets from the words on the board, and divide the class into the same number.

Tell each group to find the words on the board which fit *their* lexical set, and to build on this as much as they can, using their collective knowledge and your help.

Finally, each group presents back to the class their set of words and phrases.

Follow-up

People write an account of Jorge's wedding, using words and expressions that have emerged during the lesson.

Lightning talks

Helping each other in conversation

Think about it

'Lightning talks' are designed to prevent people from going on and on when presenting ideas – but a classroom version should help people to keep going! It focuses on an important feature of conversation: the way speakers help each other.

Get it ready

Have enough dice for each pair in the class.

Set it up

Write these discussion topics on the board, numbered as follows:

> *What I like (and don't like):*
> 1 *about my room*
> 2 *about my house*
> 3 *about my town*
> 4 *about my region*
> 5 *about my country*
> 6 *about my world*

Roll a dice and speak to the class about the topic indicated for about a minute. Don't feel you have to speak perfectly, in fact it's probably more encouraging if you hesitate and lose track: it's part of normal conversation.

Divide the class into pairs.

Let it run

- Each partner in turn rolls a dice to determine their topic. They then make some brief notes about it, before they speak. You circulate and help with language as needed.

- When people are ready, tell them to start: the first person in each pair speaks to their partner about their topic for a minute (you time this, saying when there are fifteen seconds to go). If they lose track or run out of things to say, their partner prompts them with questions.

- The partners then exchange roles, and the process is repeated.

Round it off

Each person repeats their one-minute talk for the whole class, with the support of their partner who prompts in the same way, as required, perhaps using phrases like this:

> *Didn't you say ...?   You said ...*

The focus here is fluency, but as people talk, make a note of things they have said effectively, and things they could still improve, and go through these in whole class.

Follow-up

Everyone chooses a topic for the next lesson. They prepare some ideas as homework and then work in pairs, practising their talks. Then each person gives their talk to the whole class, with their partner again prompting, as required.

Headlines

Recounting recent events in our lives

Think about it

Unplugged classes thrive on the stuff of everyday life. Why not take this detail and transform it into headline news – complete with interview questions from the class?

Get it ready

Write on a large piece of paper a 'headline' that summarises – and exaggerates – a recent event in your life. For example: *Shopping disaster, Weekend traffic horror, Tennis triumph.*

Set it up

Display the headline, and invite the class to ask you questions to get the gist of your story.

Tell the class that you want them to think of a story from *their lives*, and to write a headline for it. They should come and show you their headline before you start the activity, and you will help with language as needed.

Let it run

- The students write on a piece of paper their own headline in large, legible script.
- Half the class stand in a large circle around the room, holding their headlines so that these are clearly visible. The other half (the 'interviewers') form a second circle, inside the first one. Everyone positions themselves opposite one of the people who is holding a headline. They then ask them questions about it. You listen, and help with language.
- After a minute or so, you call out *Change!*, and the interviewers move clockwise so as to face the next headline, and begin asking questions again. This process is repeated until all the interviewers have interacted with all the headlines.
- Make any general comments that will help people as they continue the activity: these might relate to question forms, for example, or to vocabulary that is causing problems.
- The roles are then reversed: those who were doing the interviewing now stand with their own headlines and are themselves interviewed.

Round it off

Some of the most interesting stories can be reported back to the whole class. Ask people which story they enjoyed hearing about most, and why.

Follow-up

People write the story behind their own headline for homework.

My very special guest

Interviewing a visitor

Think about it

Your colleagues may be less famous than the celebrities in coursebooks, and may not hit the headlines, but they can be just as interesting for your class to talk to. They also have one big advantage over the stars: they can appear in person in the room!

Get it ready

Ask a teaching colleague, or someone else who works in the school, if they will come into your class and be interviewed (in English, though they don't have to be a very fluent speaker).

Set it up

Tell your class who is coming, and brainstorm some questions before the visit.

Write the questions on the board, and invite improvements. Make and explain adjustments of your own, as required.

Practise the questions, focusing on intonation and relevant features of connected speech, as appropriate.

Let it run

- When your colleague arrives, the class ask their questions. You encourage people to ask follow-up questions, depending on what the visitor says, and join in yourself.
- Your guest is invited to ask the class some questions in return.
- You make notes, help with language and generally encourage.

Round it off

When your guest has left, the class revisit and discuss the answers given to the questions they were asked.

Highlight and discuss any language points you noted during the question-and-answer session with your colleague.

Follow-up

Working in pairs or small groups, people write up the interview as if they were reporting it for a school magazine, local magazine or website.

Variation

If you are friendly with someone who works near the school – someone who runs a café or a bookshop, for example – you could repeat the activity with them. This will suggest a whole new range of questions. The guest doesn't need to be a fluent speaker, nor even to speak English: the class can write the questions in English and hold the interview in their first language, before translating the visitor's answers back into English.

A problem shared ...

Sharing everyday problems and solutions

Think about it

Conversations that we 'have to have' in another language often involve problems that need to be resolved; this is particularly true when learners are living in an English-speaking country.

Get it ready

Think of something that is annoying you, and be ready to talk about it in class.

Set it up

Ask the class to think of a situation or a person that is worrying or annoying them. Tell them your own 'problem'. For example: a noisy neighbour, all the homework you have to mark this weekend, the overdue library books you haven't returned.

Elicit some advice from the class, writing any phrases that are useful for giving advice on the board, refining as necessary, but without comment.

Let it run

- People stand in two parallel lines (A and B), facing each other. They take turns to relate their problem while their partner opposite listens and then offers advice.
- The student at the top of Line A moves to the bottom of the same line, and each student in that line moves up one space. They re-tell their problems to their new partners, who offer advice. This continues until everyone in Line A has interacted with everyone in Line B. They then return to their seats.
- Meanwhile, you circulate, listen and encourage, helping with language as necessary and make a note of what you help with.

Round it off

Ask the class to report on the best advice they were given. Using your notes, share the conversations you had about language with individual learners while the activity was running.

Variation

If the class size or classroom layout doesn't allow this kind of formation, the class can first do the task with their immediate partner, and then be repositioned so that they are able to interact with at least two other people successively.

... is a problem halved

Roleplaying real situations from learners' lives

Think about it

Roleplays provide practice in all the skills, and you can use real-life situations as stimulus. If people are living away from home in an English-speaking country, you may find that you can even help them prepare for tricky conversations.

Get it ready

Think about something you have recently had to deal with involving a conversation with someone: this could be anything from returning something to a store to tracing an item of mail that has gone astray, and so on.

Set it up

Tell your class about your experience, and ask if any of them have had any similar difficulties. Summarise these on the board. For example:
> *Asking for a refund*
> *Speaking to the landlord*
> *Getting permission to do something (from one's parents, teacher, boss, etc.)*

Let it run

- Working in pairs, the class prepare written roleplay dialogues in which they address a situation that is relevant to at least one of them (if neither has a situation to resolve, they should choose one from the 'pool' on the board). One role should be their own, the second role that of the person they need to speak to.
- In turn, as they finish, they show you the first draft of their roleplay. You suggest where they can adjust the language as required, and add one or two phrases that would be useful in the circumstances. Make a note of these additional phrases as you go along.
- They show you a second draft and you make any final adjustments. They read you the roleplay and you help with intonation and expression.

Round it off

Before people act out their roleplays, ask everyone to listen out for more examples of the kind of helpful phrases you have suggested.

Each pair reads out their dialogue.

Elicit all the phrases the class heard that they think would be helpful in the kind of situations being discussed. List them on the board, focus on pronunciation and explore how using different intonation can affect the 'message' you are putting across.

Follow-up

Ask if anyone has actually had the conversations they were preparing for and invite them to report back on how these went, encouraging their classmates to ask questions.

Up and down

Talking about our moods

Think about it
Sharing the way we feel about life is a fundamental element of conversation – and is also one of the key ways we build relationships.

Get it ready
Using the diagram below as an example, sketch your mood across the previous weekend. Ideally, this will show some clear ups and downs.

Set it up
Explain that you are going to talk about the weekend: about the times when you felt good or not so good, happy or less happy, or just plain bored!

Copy your diagram onto the board and explain that it shows how you felt across the weekend. Tell the class about your highs and lows as you go along, inviting and answering any questions the class may have.

Let it run
- Everyone draws a similar grid on a piece of paper, together with their own 'mood' line.
- Working in pairs, they tell each other about their weekends.
- You circulate, listen to what is being said, join in where appropriate, and note the language that is being used.

Round it off
Explore some of the words and phrases that have emerged in the course of the lesson: in addition to any naturally arising work on past verb forms, for example, you can focus on ways of expressing mood.

Follow-up
People summarise their partner's weekend in one written paragraph.

Variation
You can use the same activity to talk about a recent holiday period.

Down and up

Sharing suggestions for beating a bad mood

Think about it
Having a group of people in one place gives you the chance to pool experience and personal responses to everyday life, and this type of activity is a good way of building the social group.

Get it ready
Ask yourself the question: *How do you cheer yourself up when you're feeling down?* Have an answer ready, along with some Post-it® notes – enough for two per person, although slips of paper will work, too.

Set it up
Write the following phrase on the board:
> *When I'm feeling down, I …*

Tell people what you do to cheer yourself up when you feel down.

Let it run
- Everyone writes down how they cheer themselves up if they're feeling down, making an additional copy on a Post-it® note. You take in these notes.
- You tell the class you are going to read the notes out, one by one. Say you are going to adjust the language used as you do this, and tell people to listen out for any changes when they hear what they wrote.
- You invite them to make a final draft on another Post-it®, incorporating any changes they noticed.
- They read out the notes, and answer questions from the whole class about their own suggestions.

Round it off
Stick the revised notes to the wall and ask everyone to look over them and choose a favourite suggestion (not their own): they should mark it with a pen.

Discuss why they chose them. Which are the top three chosen by the class?

Variation
You can use the same basic procedure for sharing other kinds of advice and recommendations, such as: *good ways to save money* or *the best things to do at the weekend*, etc.

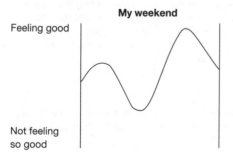

My weekend

Feeling good

Not feeling
so good

Good news, bad news

Reacting to other people's experiences

Think about it

The more your class share real news, the more important it is for them to expand their repertoire of 'reaction' phrases and learn how to use them appropriately.

Get it ready

Make a note of two things that have happened to you recently: one good, one bad. These should be relatively trivial, as you will be asking the class to make similar examples and you don't want them to feel obliged to contribute something very exciting, or to share any very bad news with the class.

Meanwhile, ask an available colleague to do the same, as you will need them at the end of the lesson!

Set it up

Tell the class your piece of good news. For example:
I finally found a CD I've been looking for.

Then tell them your piece of bad news. For example:
I tried cooking from a new recipe at the weekend, but it took me six hours and it wasn't very nice.

By using the spontaneous reactions of the class, eliciting further phrases and adding examples of your own as necessary, generate a set of 'reaction' phrases for good and bad news.

Write these on the board and practise the pronunciation, experimenting with different emphasis: the *sound* of these phrases is as important as the words themselves. (Think, for example, of the falling *ahh …* sound we use to express sympathy, or the range of responses we can express with a rising *Really?*. Even *Wow!* or *Oh no!* depend for impact on the right expression!)

Let it run

- People write down their good and bad news.
- They show them to you, and you prompt them to adjust the language as appropriate.
- Everyone reads out their examples: encourage the whole class to react at the same time. You highlight and model intonation and features of non-verbal communication, such as facial expression and body language – people are often less expressive when speaking another language. Concentrate on these with the class, and encourage an exaggerated response.

Round it off

Invite your colleague in, to tell the class their items of news: it should be fun to see their face when the whole class react – with as much (even exaggerated) expression as possible!

Variation

You can use examples from the lives of well-known people.

Slices of life

That was the week that was

Think about it

Routine information-gap activities can be personalised and adapted to focus on the people in the room.

Get it ready

There's no need to prepare anything.

Set it up

Draw a large pie chart like the one below on the board and label it *My week*.

Explain to the class that you are dividing it into three sections that indicate things you *like* doing, things you *don't mind* doing, and things you *don't like* doing (see below). Tell everyone to draw a similar chart for themselves.

Let it run

- You prompt the class to ask you about some of the things *you* like, don't mind and don't like doing.
- Someone comes to the board and fills in the sections with some of the things you like doing, don't mind doing, and don't like doing.
- The class work in pairs, asking their partner questions and filling in their partner's chart for them. You circulate and help with any language that is needed.

Round it off

Invite everyone to tell the class about their partner's week, concentrating on things they particularly like and don't like doing.

Variation

People use the same diagram to explore their enjoyment (or otherwise) of:

Different environments: home, school, work. (This is a very good way to elicit and build on workplace vocabulary for business students.)

Different periods in one's life, looking back or forward to: childhood, schooldays, retirement.

My week

41

Top three

Making a survey of everyday actions

Think about it
Details which seem mundane in isolation can be surprisingly interesting when compared with other people, and there is a lot of fun to be had sharing everyday facts about ourselves in this way.

Get it ready
There's nothing to prepare.

Set it up
Organise the class into groups of three or four. Tell them that they are going to conduct a survey to see who is the class 'slowcoach' (ie the slowest person in the class), and the class 'Speedy Gonzalez' (the fastest person).

Let it run
- In groups, they prepare five or six questions starting with the phrase: *How long ... .* For example:
    How long does it take you to get dressed in the morning?
    How long does it take you to eat breakfast?
    How long does it take you to get out of the house?
- They then circulate, asking and answering their questions and noting down the answers. You join in, helping with language and noting any words and phrases you would like to explore with the class.
- They return to their original groups to compare and collate answers, identifying the 'top three' fastest dressers, and so on.

Round it off
Finally, they report their findings to the class. Help with language as they do this, prompting a second version or adjusting input, as needed. Add any observations you have noted in the previous phase.

Variation
The same procedure can be used to find out other 'top threes', such as:
    Top three favourite things to do at the weekend
    Top three best shops in town

Hands up!

Comparing the sort of people we like best

Think about it
Differing opinions about other people are an important ingredient in everyday conversation. By working with the class and building on phrases they already know, you can generate a shared vocabulary set for describing people.

Get it ready
There's nothing to prepare.

Set it up
Ask the class to draw the outline of their two hands on a piece of paper. Tell them that the left hand represents 'people they like' and that the right hand represents 'people they don't like'.

Let it run
- On each finger of the left hand, people write an adjective that completes the sentence: *I like people who are ... .* For example, *I like people who are funny.* On each of the fingers of the right hand, they should write a negative adjective. For example: *mean*.
- Allow the class to use dictionaries, if available, and as they do the activity, you circulate and help with language as needed.
- In pairs, the class compare their 'hands', looking for similarities and differences.

Round it off
You can display these hands (labelled with the names of their owners) around the walls of the classroom. Younger learners might like to decorate them. As people circulate, encourage them to ask the 'owners' of the hands about any words they don't know, and help as necessary.

Variation
Use the same simple framework for listing *things* people like (on one hand) and dislike (on the other). For example:
    Food I like and food I dislike
    Things I like about winter and things I don't like.

Like   Don't like

One of us, none of us

Making a survey of sensory experiences

Think about it
Asking the class to make a survey is a good way to add a task element to conversations in which people share experiences they may – or may not – have had.

Get it ready
There's nothing to prepare.

Set it up
Elicit the verbs associated with the five senses: *see*, *hear*, *taste*, *smell*, and *touch*.

Let it run
- Working in small groups, each group produces at least one question of the type *Have you ever … ?*, using each of these verbs. For example: *Have you ever seen a ghost? Have you ever heard a wolf?*
- The class stand up and circulate, asking and answering the questions, and noting the answers. To do this, they will need pen and paper, and a book to support their writing on.
- You participate, make notes, help with language and generally encourage, as appropriate.

Round it off
Write the table below on the board.

When all or most of the people have interacted with each other, ask them to return to their original groups to collate the results of their survey. This should take the form of sentences like:

> *Two people have seen a ghost.*
> *None of us has eaten kangaroo meat.*

Ask a spokesperson from each group to report some of the more interesting facts they have discovered.

Follow-up
People list three experiences they hope to have one day, and then discuss what they have chosen.

Variation
This activity and table can be adapted to almost any structure, for example, starting with these question types:

> *Can you … ? (Two of us can speak Spanish.)*
> *Would you … ? (None of us would eat a rat.)*

One of us Two of us Three of us All of us None of us	has have	been to seen met eaten had *etc*	…

Plusses and minuses

Pooling likes and dislikes about everyday life

Think about it
Including a simple task element can help give focus to a conversation. You can start it with a 'set it up' suggestion, but you can also extend a conversation that has started spontaneously.

Get it ready
There's nothing to get ready.

Set it up
Tell the class about two things *you* like, and two you like less, about your job.

Tell them to note down two things *they* like, and two they like less, about their work (if they are working) – or about school/college (if they are studying).

Let it run
- Working in small groups, they share their likes and dislikes.
- Every time a group finds that two or more people have a like or dislike in common, tell them to note it on a slip of paper and pass it to you. You write a comment or question on it, and send it back (for example, if a group has noted a dislike of break times, write down how *you* feel about them, or ask what it is they don't like about them, and so on).
- They look at your comment or question, discuss it amongst themselves and continue the conversation until they have discussed all the likes and dislikes they noted.

Round it off
Using the board to make notes (you can do this yourself, or you can invite one or two people from the class to do it), summarise as a class the best and worst things about work, school/college, or both. Making two columns on the board – positive and negative – will help.

Follow-up
Ask people to write either a paragraph summarising the positives and negatives uncovered by the class, or a paragraph about their own feelings about work or school.

Variation
You can use the same process to discuss a vast range of topics and can invite people to suggest their own – anything from their families to what they think of their English class!

Last Saturday

Creating a shared narrative

Think about it

You can move from small units of text to a written narrative, and at the same time practise all the skills.

Get it ready

You will need a pair of dice for each group you form.

Set it up

Tell the class you are going back in time, to last Saturday. Explain that the dice will reveal the time. (You can start your numbering from 1 pm and go through to midnight, or – with younger learners – you can run from 1 pm to 9 pm and then have 10, 11 and 12 in the morning.)

Roll one pair of dice. Announce the time, and say what you were doing then. For example: *shopping, in the cinema, cooking dinner,* etc.

Note the time and activity on a slip of paper, add your name, and show it to the class (see the example below).

Divide the class into two groups (or four, if you have a large class) and give each group a pair of dice.

Let it run

- People roll the dice in turn. Following your example, each person writes down what they were doing at the time indicated. They then share the information with each other as a group.

- Each group exchanges all of its notes with another group. Still working as a group, people then place the notes they have been given in chronological order, and find out one more piece of information about each note (by asking the person who wrote it).

- Using their notes and the additional information, they write a narrative of the other group's day.

Round it off

Each group reads out its narrative. As they do so, note down anything relating to the handling of narrative that could be improved, such as the use of verb forms and linking words.

When they have finished, write some examples on the board and discuss with the class.

Invite the groups to make any changes to their narrative, using the examples you have discussed.

4 pm
Driving home
from the shops
Luke

Memory stars

Sharing sensory memories

Think about it

As Proust observed, sensory experiences can trigger vivid memories. We cannot rely on these experiences occurring spontaneously when we are in class, but can make up for the absence of 'madeleine' cake with a simple diagram.

Get it ready

There's nothing to prepare.

Set it up

Draw a five-pointed star on the board like the one below, and write inside the points of the star the words *sight, sound, touch, smell* and *taste.*

Ask the class to each copy the diagram onto a piece of paper. Explain that inside the first point of the star they should write a word or phrase that evokes a memorable experience involving *sight*: for example, a spectacular sunset, or a firework display. In the second point of the star, they write a word or phrase that evokes a memory involving *sound*; and so on, for the five points.

Let it run

- Using their own stars, the class write down the word or phrase they associate with that sense.

- They then form pairs or groups of three. They show one another their 'memory stars' and ask and answer questions about the experiences that each point of the star represents. For example:
  What does this mean?
  What happened to you?
  Where were you?
  How did you feel?
  What did it look/feel/taste like?

- You circulate, encourage, and ask your own questions.

Round it off

Individuals from each group report to the class something particularly interesting they heard in their conversation.

Follow-up

Ask people if there is a sixth sense. What do they understand by that? What words and experiences would people associate with the sixth sense?

You and me, from A to Zee

Creating a shared record of personal interests

Think about it

We use the A-Z for spelling practice, but it can make for an enjoyable speaking activity. This is also a good way to revise saying the alphabet in English – a useful skill that even fluent speakers can struggle to master.

Get it ready

There's nothing to prepare.

Set it up

Elicit the alphabet in sequence quickly, with each person saying one letter.

Write it on the board and focus on any difficulties that emerge, such as consonants that are not sufficiently distinguished, or vowels that are confused with first language phonemes, depending on the nationality of the learners. (You can also use this activity to practise phonics.)

Write a set of phrases, such as the following, on the board:

My favourite food
My favourite drink
My favourite singer/composer
My favourite actor/actress
My favourite sportsperson/team
My favourite pastime

Let it run

- Everyone writes down their individual answers in English, while you help with words as needed. (If you find it hard to translate a kind of food or drink, for example, leave it in the original language – it can be described in English.)

- Working in groups, people tell each other about their choices and make an A-Z, based on their collective interests. There may be more than one 'answer' for a letter (for example, two different people may have chosen *tea* and *tequila* as their favourite drink, respectively – both should be listed). You circulate, answering any questions they may have about language.

- Each group sticks their A-Zs to the wall: people look at the different versions, and everyone one notes down an entry they would like to find out more about. Make a choice of your own, too.

Round it off

In whole class, people ask who wrote the entry that caught their eye, and ask them questions about it.

Follow-up

Invite a colleague to try the same activity with their class, so you can exchange A-Zs. Each class compare these lists with their own, discuss the differences, and write down some questions for the other class. 'Post' the questions to the other class, and wait for the answers.

VIVs

Making exchange visits between classes

Think about it

All over the school, people are doing the same thing as you: communicating and trying to improve their English. Why not make contact with them?

Get it ready

Arrange with a colleague for learners from your respective classes to make 'exchange visits' during a lesson.

Set it up

Tell your class that two people from another class, two Very Important Visitors (VIVs), will be joining you for part of the lesson, and that two people from your class will be joining the other class in return.

Explain that they are going to 'interview' the visitors.

Let it run

- Brainstorm a set of questions about the visitors' lives, likes and dislikes, and write them on the board as they are elicited. Then adjust them for accuracy as a whole-class exercise.

- Once you have welcomed your VIVs (and your own two VIVs have left for the other class), you start the question-and-answer session.

- You and your class can encourage longer answers by using prompts like this:
  That's interesting – tell us more.
  Is that typical of your friends/family ... your town/country?

  You can also shift conversation to the other person, like this:
  What about you?
  Is it the same for you?

Round it off

Once your visitors have left, explain that you want the class to write 'pen-portraits' of the people they have interviewed. The pen-portraits should describe who they are, what they enjoy, and so on.

Divide the class into pairs, labelling the people in each pair *A* and *B*: the As should write a pen-portrait of one visitor, and the Bs of the other.

Ask the pairs to compare descriptions, suggesting anything they think has been left out.

Follow-up

Send the pen-portraits to the other class, in exchange for their descriptions of your students.

Alternatively, the respective VIVs can be invited back, and the classes read out the pen-portraits you have written, asking if they think they are accurate.

Three wishes

Drawing up a personal wish list

Think about it

It usually works in fairy tales, but asking people to 'think of three wishes' in real life, out of the blue, can draw a blank. It can help if you use a visual framework that gives prompts and includes an element of choice.

Get it ready

Try the setting up yourself before class, drawing five concentric circles as outlined below and thinking of a wish for three of these circles or 'dimensions'.

Set it up

Draw five large concentric circles on the board. In the inner circle, write *Me*, then *My family and friends*, then *My work/school*, then *My town/neighbourhood*, and in the outermost circle, *The world*.

Ask the students to copy this diagram on a piece of paper and to write down a wish for three of these circles. Demonstrate this by giving examples of your own:

(Me) *It would be nice to have a day off.*
(My family and friends) *I'd like to see my aunt this weekend.*
(My town) *I wish they would sort out the buses.*

Let it run

- The class work on their circles individually, thinking of a wish for three of the dimensions.
- They show you their draft statements. You help with language as required, and they adjust accordingly.
- In small groups, people exchange their circles and respond to each other's wishes, asking questions and discussing any similarities or differences of opinion. You circulate, encourage (for example, by asking questions of your own) and help with language, as required.

Round it off

The class has to adopt a single 'wish' for their town. First, each group discusses and chooses one to submit to the whole class. You write these on the board and the class discuss, with each group arguing for their own wish.

Finally, people come to the board and tick their favourite wish. The winner is the one with the most votes.

Repeat for *The world*.

The perfect school

Brainstorming ideas for improvements

Think about it

We sometimes think of imaginary scenarios as being remote from reality – but they are often closely linked to the changes we want to make in our lives.

Get it ready

There's nothing to prepare.

Set it up

Tell the class you are going to write a word on the board, and that you want them to tell you what they immediately associate with that word.

Write up the word *school*. As people call out their associations, note them around the word, without comment.

Talk about some of the positives, some of the negatives.

Divide the class into groups, and ask each group to nominate a 'scribe'. Tell them they are going to share ideas for 'the perfect school'.

Let it run

- In groups, people use the same process to brainstorm ideas for the perfect school, with the scribe writing down the others' ideas. Set a time limit for this.
- Each group decides on the five changes they would like to make. They draw up their plan on a piece of paper, listing the five improvements in headline form (for example: *A bigger café*) and the reason why each one is a good idea (*It would make it easier for people to socialise*).
- You look over each group's plan, suggesting adjustments that will make the language more appropriate for its purpose.

Round it off

In open class, each group comes to the front of the class and presents their plan for the perfect school, sticking their plan to the board.

Everyone gets up and looks at the plans, before finally voting for their favourite three recommendations.

Follow-up

In pairs, people draft a letter to the director of the school, asking if the suggested improvements can be made. They read out their letters.

Using phrases from these drafts, and adding any phrases of your own that suggest themselves, build a composite letter on the board – discussing this with the class as you go along. Copy it out, and 'send' it. Wait and see if you get a reply. If there is more to say on the subject, or there are any unanswered questions – draft a further letter together.

Desert island

Making a short list for a long trip

Think about it
This popular discussion topic is always fun, as it involves talking about ourselves. This version uses a simple framework to guarantee participation and debate.

Get it ready
Ask yourself what *you* would take to a desert island. You are allowed one kind of food or drink, one book and one CD. Make a mental note of your own choices.

Set it up
Ask the class to imagine they are going to live on a pleasant but remote desert island for a year. What would be good about it? What would be bad about it?

Tell them they will be living on their own, and that they must choose one kind of food or drink, one book and one CD, to take with them.

Hand out some slips of paper.

Let it run
- Everyone writes down their three choices on a single piece of paper, without showing it to anyone else (and without writing their name on it). They fold up these pieces of paper, and put them into a box. You do the same.

- You shake up the pieces of paper and redistribute them, asking people to take one from the box and telling them to refold and replace the piece of paper if they pick their own.

- The class mingles. By telling each other what is listed on their piece of paper, without showing it, people have to find the author of the note they have picked out of the box. When they find them, they must ask them about their choices. You circulate, encouraging and helping with language as required.

Round it off
Sitting down again, in open class, people interview the same person about their choices – effectively repeating the conversation they have just had, but including any language you have supplied.

Variation
After writing down their three choices, people keep their own slip of paper and mingle, trying to find someone whose choices are similar or at least compatible with their own – so they can share the desert island! They can ask questions like: *What would you like to eat?* etc., until they find the person with the most suitable matches.

Where I'd rather be

Imagining ourselves elsewhere

Think about it
However much we enjoy teaching or learning, it's just possible that school wouldn't be our first choice of place to be on any given day. Using a simple framework can help people to articulate the alternatives.

Get it ready
There's nothing to prepare.

Set it up
Draw a triangle on the board like the one below and write at each point the following questions:
> *Where would you rather be?*
> *Who would you rather be with?*
> *What would you rather be doing?*

Invite the class to ask you these questions, and ask someone to note your answers on the board as you go.

Answer any further questions they may have, refining the language and writing on the board any useful question structures that emerge, such as:
> *Who's/Where's/What's that?*
> *Why would you rather be with him/her?*
> *Why would you rather be there/doing that?*

Let it run
- People draw their own triangles, writing one or two-word answers to the questions.

- Working in pairs or groups of three, people look at each other's triangles and ask questions about them.

- You circulate, encouraging and helping with language.

Round it off
Ask different people to report to the class any particularly interesting information they learned.

Tell people to work in pairs to suggest something else that the *whole class* might enjoy doing.

Take in the answers, read them out to the class and discuss the alternatives.

Finally, everyone writes down their favourite. You count up the votes and announce the winner.

Follow-up
See if you can organise a class social event – it might not be the equivalent of the alternative they have chosen, but it can be enjoyable and worthwhile to meet up outside class.

47

Selecting stimulus to share

We come across all sorts of 'things' that we want to share with other people in the course of the day, from stories in the news to things we see in the street.

We often have a good idea of who we're going to share these things with: 'I must tell X about that', or 'I've got to show that to Y'. If you think of your class in the same way, you will start noticing things that may interest them – and you can encourage them to do the same.

The things you find – objects, images and texts – will become your unplugged materials. They can be used to start conversations, to introduce a variety of text types and to incorporate learner suggestions.

These materials are 'free' in two senses of the word: not only can they be freely sourced from the local environment, but they also allow lessons to grow naturally from the initial stimulus. The less prescriptive your lesson is in terms of outcomes, the more productive it will be.

Although there are no photocopiable lessons here, these activities are easy to prepare. It's less about looking for specific things, and more about keeping an eye open for what might be interesting. Materials shouldn't be hard for you to find, or too time-consuming for the class to process. It's what happens next that counts.

Lessons on location

Before you look outside the classroom for stimulus, think of what can be used inside it. Even if you don't have a room with a view, you can invite people to close their eyes and imagine themselves elsewhere. The classroom floor can be cleared and used to represent a different space – from your town to the world. Classroom decoration you might not think twice about can also be stimulating if looked at from a different angle: an old map of the world that's been there for years will still unlock your learners' imagination.

Lessons in your pocket

Some of the best lessons involve *no text* at all to begin with, and activities might use physical objects that you can easily find and bring to school, or which are already part of the learners' lives. Whole lessons can grow from the *smallest* of objects, given life by the learners' responses, and shaped by your attention to the language that emerges.

Involve your class, too. The more you engage them in thinking about their English *between* lessons, the more receptive to learning opportunities they will become. Setting homework that involves finding stimulus to bring into class is very motivating because it sets up expectations of what is going to happen when they share it with other people.

Use the news

A well-chosen article from a current English language newspaper or website will generate conversation, whilst also providing a ready-made focus on form. You can also take text apart, creating information gaps and imaginative diversions. And whether or not it's in English, there's plenty more you can do with the news: cut out the pictures, fix the pages to the walls – and see what catches the imagination of the class.

Take a text

Text changes, from the moment it is conceived to the point at which it is expressed. It changes when it is read or heard; it changes when it is reported. Activities which reflect this changeable nature can provide real insight into the way text is constructed and decoded. You can start with tiny amounts of text; you can start with text from the most transient and apparently insignificant sources. And, as with conversation, texts that are relevant to your learners' lives can provide the most engaging stimulus of all.

Selecting stimulus to share

Tips and techniques

1 Choose stimulus that can be processed quickly by the class, leading directly to discussion or language work. Non-verbal stimulus and tactile things that can be passed around the room are particularly immediate.

2 When using non-verbal stimulus, don't worry about predicting what your students will make of it. They might not think of the things that occurred to *you*, and they will almost certainly think of things that you *didn't*. Keep an open mind, and see how they respond: this will make it much more interesting for you, and much more worthwhile for them.

3 Stimulus can range from objects to texts to living people, and in some cases can be sourced online or captured by mobile phone. If you and your class have ready access to these technologies, use them: if not, it doesn't matter, there's always an alternative.

4 If you *are* working with text, choose examples that are short enough to be written on the board and copied down, or dictated to the class. This time is not wasted: people are already processing language, and setting aside a little quiet time for copying can be calming.

5 Avoid using texts that demand a lot of background knowledge, and decide beforehand what to do with any vocabulary that might prove difficult. You can leave it out, replace it with a simpler word, or invite students to deduce the meaning from the context.

6 Choose your text according to how much you think it will interest your class: the language generated *by* a text is often more important than the language *in* it.

7 Sharing stimulus that you have found yourself has a social dimension, as there will always be a 'story', no matter how small, to how it was found: *I was just outside my house fixing my car when this man came up with a flyer for a new pizza place.* This incidental detail can add to the charm of finding materials for free.

8 Demonstrate your willingness to explore *real* language examples, and encourage people in the class to bring in examples of their own. Even when invited to, some may do this but some may not – especially at first. Don't worry about this: rather, try and build enthusiasm from those that do.

9 Saving something up for a lesson doesn't mean that you *have* to use it in class. If conversation develops spontaneously in another direction, save the material you have found for another day. Don't keep it too long, though – the freshness is important. Something you found that morning will be more engaging for you and the class than something dated or that you have used before. And remember: something that was hugely successful with one class may, sadly, fizzle out quickly with another.

10 Be patient! Things can take a while to get going, and it's important to give people the time and space to respond, generate and organise ideas. Unplugged teaching demands considerable trust, but if you demonstrate faith in the learners' capacity to think for themselves, it will be repaid.

Selecting stimulus means searching beyond the staffroom for what will get people talking:

- **Images** – stimulus doesn't need to involve text to begin with.
- **Objects** – things from the immediate surroundings, to handle and pass round.
- **Texts** – the shorter, the better.

Involve your class in finding things to *share*. Together, you can:

- **Mine the media** – finding images and text in print or online.
- **Collect things** – from flyers and packaging, letters and e-mails, to the wording on a bus ticket.
- **Be pro-active** – using what you have to hand (from pen and paper to mobile phones) to make notes, take pictures and record sound.

'Real' world

Using the classroom space to make a map

Think about it

Adding a fun element to a task can help people to relax. People can act as physical prompts for one another, adding a spatial dimension to a speaking activity.

Get it ready

Clear a space on the classroom floor, if possible with the help of the class, by moving as much furniture as possible to the walls.

Set it up

Tell the class that the classroom floor is a map of the world. Use the walls to establish north, south, east and west. Ask people to estimate where in the world the classroom is, and mark this with some object. Between you, agree the position of one or two capital cities for further orientation.

Let it run

- Everyone stands in a location that represents a place they would like to visit.

- Using only questions that can be answered with *yes* or *no*, people have to guess where each person is standing. You can join in, asking example *yes/no* questions, such as:

    Are you in a city?
    Are you on an island?
    Can you see lots of people where you are?

- Everyone tells the class something they can *see*, something they can *hear* and something they can *smell*.

Round it off

People try to persuade each other to come to their location. If anyone one *does* move to someone else's location, ask what persuaded them to do so.

Variation

Depending on who is in your class, use the same process to create a map of places people are from, or have actually visited.

Alternatively, make it a map of their country or city.

Re-view

Mapping our memories

Think about it

A memory can be as vivid as a physical picture and just as stimulating, because it draws directly on people's own experience.

Get it ready

There's nothing to prepare.

Set it up

Describe a view that you remember clearly – it could be a view you remember from a particular time in your life, or a view you particularly love.

Let it run

- People think of a view that they are familiar with and that has 'special' associations. For example: the view from their bedroom window, or a place where they once spent a holiday. Everyone notes three things they remember particularly clearly about this view.

- In pairs, they take turns to describe the view to their partner, who can ask questions about it. You circulate, encouraging and helping with language as appropriate.

- Each person then attempts to describe the scene back to the original student, who evaluates its accuracy.

Round it off

Everyone tells the class about their partner's view.

As they do this, note on the board one or two key phrases from their descriptions, pointing out any adjustments you have made to improve them.

Follow-up

People write a description of a favourite view. When they have shown it to you and you have suggested some improvements (these could be to do with accuracy, style or expression), invite everyone to read out their description to the class.

Variation

As an alternative to the basic process, the partner can attempt to *draw* the scene.

Destination unknown

Using a map as creative stimulus

Think about it
Many classrooms use maps as decoration. If your classroom has one, or there is one somewhere else in school (for example, in an atlas), you can use it for a fun writing activity.

Get it ready
Find a map of the world in school – the larger the better.

Set it up
Gather the class around the map. Explain that everyone is going on a 'magical mystery tour' to somewhere different on earth, and that they won't know where they are until they have arrived.

Let it run
- Ask who wants to go first: this person closes their eyes and, using the non-writing end of a pen as a 'pin', places it at random on the map. They can now open their eyes: this is where they are going for their trip.
- You elicit and refine a working definition of where they have landed. For example:
  Somewhere in the middle of the Indian Ocean
  Just outside Wroclaw
  In the far north of Canada
- They write this down, and you repeat the process until everyone has discovered and noted their mystery destination.
- Working individually, people draft a postcard or SMS text from their location, telling the class something about their surroundings but without stating where they are. They show you the first draft and you suggest where it might be improved, or help them to make adjustments, as appropriate. They complete a second draft to share with the class.

Round it off
Take in the postcards/texts and redistribute them at random. People read the one they have been given and guess who sent it, and from where.

As a whole class, discuss who is happiest/least happy with their location.

Share some of the improvements and adjustments you suggested with the whole class.

Follow-up
People tell the story of how they got home. This can be done as a piece of creative writing, or in the form of an interview with the class for which each person prepares by writing down five key 'facts' about their journey.

Twin trips

Sharing local knowledge

Think about it
We all build up knowledge of the town or country we live in, and you can use a map to prompt people to share this.

Get it ready
Find a large map of the town or country where you're teaching, and select some disparate locations – one for each person in the class, including you. Note these on individual slips of paper, and fold them. Jumble them up and number them.

Set it up
Gather the class around the map. Tell them they will all be given their location, and that they will be working with a partner to find the best way to reach each other.

Invite people to choose one of the slips of paper. Before they open it, they should use their number to find a partner: 1 pairs with 2, 3 with 4, and so on. As always, you make up the last pair if the people in the room make up an odd number.

Let it run
- Working with their partner, people find their locations on the map. You help out if people are 'lost'.
- Returning to their seats and working individually, each person plans how they would travel to where the other person is.
- When they have done this, they get into their pairs again and compare their travel plans, deciding on the best way to make the journey.

Round it off
Write on the board the following questions for people to consider during the subsequent discussion:
Which was the shortest/longest journey?
Which journey would be the most/least enjoyable?
Which would be the cheapest/most expensive?
How many different means of transport were involved?

Everyone tells the class about the journeys they have decided to make.

In pairs, people decide on the answers to the questions, and you then discuss these as a class.

Variation
This activity can also be done with a map of the world, which makes it a more imaginative (even fantastic) activity.

Matchbox magic

Generating vocabulary from minimal stimulus

Think about it
Making something out of nothing (or next to nothing!) is very satisfying. You can start with a single small piece of stimulus and go wherever the learners take it.

Get it ready
Find a matchbox or similar small container. Place a small object such as a coin inside, and bring it to class.

Set it up
Pass the matchbox round the class. Ask each person to look inside, without showing anyone else, and to write down the first thing that they associate with that object on a Post-it® note or slip of paper.

Let it run
- People mingle and compare what they have written with the rest of the class, looking for similar reactions. They group themselves according to their reactions; groups can be large or small.

- As they do this, you circulate and ask them why they have grouped themselves in this way, helping with language as needed.

- Each group develops its notes into three statements about the stimulus, and shares their statements with the whole class. You encourage and help people to develop interesting areas in a whole-class discussion.

Round it off
Using the statements, develop lexical fields under these headings:

Fact (*What is it?*)
Function (*What does it do?*)
Feeling (*How do people feel about it?*)

Follow-up
People write down an answer to at least one of the following questions:

If you were going to do something good/bad with this thing, what would it be?

If you were going to give it to someone, who would it be? Why?

If you were going to change something about it, what would it be? Why?

Variation
You could use one of the following, or anything else you find: a stamp; a leaf; a flower; a grain of rice; a feather; a ring-pull; a seashell; a sweet; a lottery ticket; an aspirin; a key; a marble; some sand; some sugar.

You can, of course, ask your students to bring things in themselves.

Good things, bad things

Using physical stimulus to generate debate

Think about it
Stimulus doesn't have to be rich or strange to get people talking, and even the most familiar objects can be used to start a free-flowing conversation.

Get it ready
Find some iconic symbol of modern life (perhaps avoiding true icons such as religious books). For example, it could be a well known soft drink can, a mobile phone or a computer mouse.

Set it up
Place the object in front of the class. Tell everyone to write down one thing that is positive about it, and one thing that is negative.

Let it run
- Working in pairs, the class compare and discuss their responses.

- You draw a line down the middle of the board or a large sheet of paper. Mark it *Good* on one side, and *Bad* on the other.

- The class come and write down their *good* and *bad* associations.

- When everyone has done this, they discuss as a whole class. You can prompt people to say more by asking questions:
    Mario, you said ... Can you tell us more?
    What do other people think? Does anyone agree or disagree?

Round it off
Say that one end of the room represents more positive feelings about the stimulus. Say that the other end of the room represents more negative feelings.

Invite everyone to go to the end of the room that represents how they feel.

Tell the people who have gathered in each part of the room to prepare an argument.

Debate the issue: the aim is to see if they can persuade anyone to come to their side of the room.

Follow-up
Repeat the activity, using objects chosen by the class and brought into school.

Variation
If you can, link up with a colleague so each of you does the same activity. If you use a large sheet of paper to write down the class responses, these can be exchanged: each class can compare their responses with those of the other.

Pocket Pecha Kucha*

Talking about the things we carry round with us

Think about it
Pecha Kucha is a 'show and tell' presentation technique that was devised to stop designers from talking too much about their ideas! Adapted for the classroom, it can encourage people to talk *more*.

Get it ready
There's nothing to prepare.

Set it up
Explain that everyone will be 'telling' the class about themselves, but that they will be doing this by showing objects.

Tell them to find three things on their person, in their pockets or in a bag, that 'say' something about their lifestyle, personality or interests. For example: a ring or chain, a book or music player, a photo, some food, etc.

Let it run
- The first person displays their objects, showing each one for twenty seconds in turn.
- When they have finished, the class ask that person questions about the objects they chose to display.
- You make notes, help with language and generally encourage, as appropriate. This continues until everyone has spoken and been interviewed.

Round it off
Tell people to work in pairs and to write something about their partner's objects, before checking with their partner that what they have written is accurate.

Everyone makes a final copy on a Post-it® note, which can be displayed on the walls and browsed by the whole class.

Variation
You can use the same process to stimulate people to talk about their hobbies or interests by adding a homework task element. Everybody brings to school three items that relate to a hobby or interest, and displays it in the way described above.

* **Pecha Kucha** was devised by Astrid Klein and Mark Dytham in Tokyo in 2003. The name derives from a Japanese term for the sound of conversation ('chit-chat').

Secret treat

Buying yourself a little something as homework

Think about it
Homework doesn't have to involve 'language work': people can prepare for the next lesson by looking for stimulus and bringing it in.

Get it ready
Invite everyone to buy something small for themselves – the sort of thing they would buy to give themselves a little 'treat' – and bring it to the next lesson. Set a price limit, and set it low. It can be anything at all, but it must be something they will enjoy, and they must keep it secret. Tell them you will do the same.

Bring a large bag to school.

Set it up
Ask people to place their item inside the large bag as they arrive. Don't forget to add your own.

Then invite each person to pick something out of the bag at random. If it's theirs, they shouldn't say!

Let it run
- In turn, each person describes the item they have taken.
- You help with language, noting relevant words or phrases on the board.
- People guess who bought the items. If the person they have guessed didn't buy it, this person then takes on the task of guessing who did!

Round it off
Invite everyone to say why they chose their item for themselves. See what language emerges, and help by adjusting, highlighting and focusing on form, as appropriate.

Follow-up
In a subsequent lesson, people see how many 'treats' (matched to the name of the purchaser) they can remember and what they can remember of the explanations.

Variation
Display the items where everyone can see them – on a table, or even on the floor.

The class observe the items in silence, making a list of what they see and who they think has bought it for themselves, asking for help if they can't find a word.

When everyone has finished, they compare their lists and guesses with a partner.

Finally, you hold up each item in turn: people describe it, before finding out if their guess was correct.

Snapshots

Creating a diary between classes

Think about it

Mobile phones are increasingly part of everyday life around the world. If everyone in your class has a mobile phone, why not make use of them? But the principle of using a phone to 'snap' something can be extended to note-taking, so the technology isn't essential.

Get it ready

Explain that everyone will be contributing to a visual diary of the time between classes, by taking a 'snapshot' of something they do, or a place they go, and bringing it to the next class. They can collect some physical evidence of something they have seen (such as a leaflet), or take an actual picture on their mobile phone.

Set it up

Ask everyone to get their 'snapshot' ready.

Let it run

- In turn, people show the class what they have snapped. If possible, hand it round the class.
- People ask questions about it, finding out when and where it was taken. You make notes, help with language and generally encourage, as appropriate.
- Divide the class into two groups (if the class is small, you won't need to do this). Ask them to put their snapshots in chronological order, and to write a narrative of the time between classes. For example:
  At 4 pm Jorge was in a museum and picked up a leaflet.
  At 8.30 pm Akiko saw a sunset and took a photo.

Round it off

Each group reads out their narrative and answers any questions from the other group.

You feed back on the learner language you noted earlier.

Follow-up

Encourage people to take 'snapshots' like this whenever they want to share something with the class, and invite them to display and talk about them at the start of a lesson.

Soundshots

Using home-made recordings

Think about it

Small, portable recording devices – from Walkmen to mobile phones – enable people to make recordings as they go about their daily life. If you have access to one, it can be used to create stimulus from the local environment.

Get it ready

Using a mobile phone or portable voice recorder, make short recordings of the ambient sound in from three to five different places over the weekend. These could be places like a train station, a café, a party, a park, a sports event, and so on.

Set it up

Tell the class you are going to tell them the story of your weekend in sound, by playing some recordings you made in different places you went to. Tell them you will play them in order – from the first you recorded, to the last.

Divide the class into pairs.

Let it run

- You play the sound recordings, pausing between each one. After each recording, people decide in their pairs where the sound was recorded.
- After the last recording, and working individually, they write down a short account of your weekend, stating the places they think you went to, in the order they heard them.
- People then compare their accounts, in pairs.

Round it off

Tell the class the locations you went to, writing these on the board as you go, and ask how many they got right. Answer any questions they may have (such as why you were there, etc.).

Then ask what sounds gave them the clues to the location. Help with the language, building up a vocabulary set as you go along.

Variation

If your learners have access to a mobile phone or other recording equipment, ask them to make their own recordings to play to the class. Perhaps you can arrange with the school to have a 'shared' device, and allow different people to use it when they want to.

Wall-papers

Reading a newspaper together

Think about it
We think of reading the papers as an individual activity, but it doesn't have to be. Why not get people on their feet and talking, allowing the class to choose what looks most interesting in the newspaper?

Get it ready
Get hold of a newspaper, in English or any other language – the more recent, the better. Have some Post-it® notes or some slips of paper ready.

Set it up
Spread the pages around the class, attaching them to the walls, and give everyone two Post-it® notes. Tell people to write their name on each of the notes. If you can, play some background music.

Let it run
- Everyone walks around the room, browsing the pages on view.
- When they see a text or image that interests them, they stick a Post-it® note next to it – whether or not someone has already done the same. (The class may not be speaking much at this point, but plenty of language processing will be going on – this is a good early-morning activity!)
- You circulate, adding some stickers of your own. People can move theirs as they go along, if they see something more interesting.

Round it off
Starting with the item that has most stickers, discuss the images or texts in whole class. In each case, ask someone who chose it to explain why they found it interesting, ensuring that everyone has a chance to describe something.

Note examples of successful (and less successful) usage as you do this, and go through these with the class – make sure you have an example from each speaker, or from as many as possible.

Follow-up
Everyone summarises their articles or photos in a single sentence. Framework sentences can help here, such as: *It's an article about X, and how Y.*

For example: *It's an article about **the England football** team, and how **they lost to Russia**.*

Variation
Try using other text types, such as information leaflets or marketing brochures. This can be a good way of alerting learners to any English language resources that are freely available.

Every picture tells a story

Generating text from a single image

Think about it
There's nothing simpler than putting a picture on the wall as stimulus: everything else flows from the learners.

Get it ready
Find a current newspaper or news magazine, and choose a photograph from the cover or – provided it's a large picture – from inside. You'll also need a large piece of paper – big enough to cover half of the board.

Set it up
Without saying anything, display the photo so the class can see it – though not on the board, which you will need.

Let it run
- Still without saying anything, you wait for the class to speak. Allow them to get over any initial hesitation: words, phrases or sentences will follow.
- Once they have started speaking, you invite someone to come and write, on the *left* side of the board, the 'story' of the picture – as jointly constructed by the class. At this point, explain that you are going to leave the room and that you will come back when they have finished.
- The class finish the story of the picture. You put your head round the door to keep track of their progress, but don't come back in until they say they are ready.

Round it off
On the *right* side of the board, reformulate the learners' text, explaining any significant changes.

Once you have discussed the new text together, cover it up with a large piece of paper. Working in pairs, people reconstruct the reformulated text in groups, before comparing it with the version on the board and making adjustments to their version, as necessary.

Follow-up
Ask the learners to bring a photo of their choosing to class for the next lesson. Depending on how many people bring a photo in, you can spread the activity over more than one lesson. Alternatively, if you do this activity once a week, you could ask a different learner to bring a photo of their choice each time.

Secret meeting

Being creative with newspaper pictures

Think about it

One advantage that a newspaper has over a book is that it can be cut up. You can do this with both text or images: here, pictures are used as a prompt for dialogues.

Get it ready

Tear out a large number of pictures of people from a newspaper or magazine. You need to have an individual face for each person in the class. Aim for a variety of types: men and women, old and young, some famous, some not.

Number each picture.

Also, number and fold some small slips of paper. You will need one number per person.

Set it up

Put the photos into a box and invite people to pick one at random.

Pick out the folded numbers two by two, announcing pairs: *Number 3 … with number 15*, and so on.

People have to mingle until they find their pair.

Let it run

- Everyone sits down with their partner. Each pair now has two pictures, and they have to decide why the two people in their pictures are having a secret meeting at a nearby café at that very moment.

- They develop a dialogue between the two people which reveals their reason for meeting, and write it down.

- You read their first draft, suggest improvements, and then read the second draft.

Round it off

The pairs show the class the pictures and read out their dialogues.

Variation

Tear out images of *people* and simply distribute at random. Everyone has to explain how they came to be seen in a café with that person when they were supposed to be in class.

Tear out images of *places*. Distribute at random. Everyone has to explain why they were *there* instead of in class.

Echoes

Comparing two versions of a news story

Think about it

News stories travel the world in hours online, making it easy to find different versions of English language texts if you have access to the internet.

Get it ready

Find an engaging news story, and enter a detail from the story (for example, someone's name) into an internet search engine. Print or copy out two versions of the same story.

Set it up

Put the two versions of the text up on opposite walls. Mark one *A* and the other *B*.

Divide the class into pairs – one person in each pair will be *A*, and one *B*.

Let it run

- The partners in each pair independently do their own 'running dictation':

  The As go and look at their text, memorising a phrase and then writing it down, until they have finished.

  The Bs do the same with their text.

- Everyone double-checks their completed version.

- Each pair compares the two versions, identifying the following:

  The longest piece of identical text

  As many identical collocations as they can

  Any differences between the two texts – additions or omissions

Round it off

Remove the two versions, and tell each pair to recreate the text, using input from both versions.

Follow-up

If the class can go online, they see if they can find any more versions of the same text and bring these to the next lesson for discussion.

Mind the gap

Using the lead sentence of a news story as stimulus

Think about it

Coursebooks often require people to decode large amounts of text before they start to discuss or answer questions about it. Yet you can generate both discussion and questions from a single sentence, proceeding either to a fuller version of the original text or to an imaginative continuation of it. News stories, with their concise sentence structure and density of information, are ideal.

Get it ready

Find a news story whose opening line contains a curious fact or twist of some sort. There is one at the bottom of this page.

Set it up

Dictate the first sentence of the story, replacing a key word or phrase with 'blank'. In our example:

A man of 80 who stole £365,000 from his ailing wife and spent it on [blank] has been jailed for two years.

Let it run

- People write down their suggestion for the missing word or phrase, without showing it to one another.

- One person dictates the sentence back to you, without filling in the blank. You write the sentence on the board, making adjustments as necessary. Other people call out their suggestions for the blank, then you reveal the original phrase.

- People work in pairs or groups and think of questions they would like to have answered by the rest of the text. Write these questions on the board.

Round it off

Dictate the rest of the text, and allow people to discuss the answers to their questions. Were they all answered?

Finally, ask a different person to dictate back to you each sentence. Explore any differences between this and the original, adjusting the class version as appropriate.

Follow-up

The class rewrite the text by either using their original suggestion for the gap-fill, or substituting detail, such as characters and place names, from their own country or region for the ones in the original story.

Note the numbers

An instant listening comprehension

Think about it

Numbers are often at the heart of a news story – ages of protagonists, time and dates of incidents, amounts of money, and so on. By isolating the numbers from a text and tasking listeners with working out their significance to the story, you can easily make a compelling comprehension task from the day's news.

Get it ready

Using a short text like the one below, isolate some of the numbers and jumble them up.

Set it up

Write the numbers on the board, in a different order from which they appear in the text. Tell people to copy them down.

Tell the class that they will hear all of these numbers mentioned during a text: their challenge is to work out their significance/what they mean in the story.

Let it run

- As you read the full text, at slow-to-medium speed, people individually match the numbers to elements within the story (for example, *the watch* was worth £1,000; *David Cryer* was 80 years old, etc.) and make notes.

- They compare their ideas with a partner, and you read out the text again.

- Working in groups or pairs, they use their notes to write a reconstruction of the text.

Round it off

Each group or pair reads out their version of the story.

Finish by reading out the original text and checking for comprehension.

Variation

Divide the class into groups and give each group a number. They each listen out for their number, note its significance to the story, and then put their ideas together in whole class.

You can also isolate the names of *people* or *places*, and ask the learners to establish their significance and role within the story.

The Star, **Monday October 15th 2007**

A man of 80 who stole £365,000 from his ailing wife and spent it on a younger woman has been jailed for two years.

Lovesick David Cryer treated Maureen Edwards, 53, to holidays, a car and a £1,000 watch.

But days after buying her a £167,000 cottage in Loughborough, Leicester, Maureen left him – and later told cops he was a 'silly old fool'.

Predicting the original text

Imagining a text from a just a summary

Think about it

Texts are often used as initial stimulus – to kick off a coursebook unit, or as a source of example forms and lexis. But you can also make a text the end-point of an activity by providing your class with a summary outline, and asking them to imagine – and to write – the text themselves.

Get it ready

Choose a text that will have some relevance to your learners, whether because of the content or because the text type corresponds to one your learners may encounter in an examination. You can vary the text type and complexity to suit the abilities of your class.

Think of how you can usefully summarise its style and content. If it helps, make a note of this summary, using the headings suggested below.

Set it up

Tell the class you are going to describe a text to them, and that you want them to try to imagine the actual text.

Write up the following on the board:
  Title
  Type of text
  Names of people or places
  Length of text (in number of words, as a guide only)
Tell the class about:
  The style of the text
Finally, describe and suggest that they note down:
  The most important pieces of information in the text

Let it run

• Working individually, the class draft a written version of the text as they imagine it.

• They compare their draft with a partner and borrow any ideas they think will improve their own draft. You circulate, encourage and help them to express their ideas.

• Read out the original text, and invite them to make any changes they want to make to their draft. Invite initial comment; explaining that you will answer any specific questions later.

Round it off

Fix the text to the board and ask people to come and compare their version with the original.

Discuss and answer any questions they have about language.

Follow-up

A similar text type is described and constructed in a subsequent lesson. The class compare the two original texts after they have completed the activity, to identify similarities.

A question of content

Home-made reading comprehension

Think about it

If your class have access to the internet (this might be at school or at home), you can invite them to find, and print or copy out, stories they would like to share, and get them to write their own comprehension questions about these texts for the class to answer. Newspapers (see the Variation) can also be used.

Get it ready

For homework, ask your class to go online and find a text. It doesn't need to be a long text, just something that interests them. It doesn't even have to be in English, provided the questions and answers are. It can be anything from a song lyric to an extract from online chat. Find a text of your own.

Set it up

Hold up the text you have chosen, tell the class what it is and say something about why you chose it, without reading it out or describing the content in detail.

Ask everyone, in turn, to hold up their text and do the same.

Let it run

• Everyone writes comprehension questions in English about their own text. You check these, suggesting adjustments as you go, and noting examples of successful and less successful use.

• Working in pairs, people exchange texts and questions with a partner, and write answers to the comprehension questions they have been given.

• Partners check one another's answers, while you circulate and answer any questions they may have.

Round it off

Write on the board a selection of the notes you have made. Don't forget to include examples of both successful and less successful usage.

Ask people to identify the ones that could be improved, and discuss ways of doing this.

Variation

You can use the same process by giving everyone in class a page from a newspaper – in any language – and asking them to write questions about an article on their page. Provided the questions and answers are in English, it doesn't matter if the paper is in their first language.

Predicting the text type
Exploring different sources

Think about it

We encounter all sorts of different texts every day. Bringing real examples to class means that there will be a story behind the stimulus, adding to the interest of exploring the features that differentiate one kind of text from another.

Get it ready

Select some varied texts, and choose a sentence from each that gives a flavour of the text type. If possible, bring the actual texts to school – if you have taken a sentence from an SMS text or a poster in the street, note it on a slip of paper.

Set it up
Write the sentences on the board.

Let it run
- Working in small groups, people try to guess what kind of text the sentences are from. Elicit guesses from the class, adjusting their description of different text types (flyer, brochure, letter, text, etc.) as necessary, before you write them on the board.
- Write the actual text types along the top of a board – the learners check their guesses against these, and you confirm the correct matches.
- You hand out the original texts. As they pass these round, the class discuss these questions in groups:
  Who created this text?
  What did they want the reader to do as a result?
  What 'tone of voice' did they use in the text?

Round it off
Discuss the answers, focusing on the language elements that helped decide which text was which.

Highlight these, and discuss as appropriate.

Variation

Invite the learners to bring in examples of their own. If enough people bring examples, you can prepare the activity in the same way, using *their* input.

Examples encountered by the authors

Bring sunshine to your table with the new alfresco summer pizza. (Flyer for local pizzeria)
We hope your child will learn and have fun and this brochure will be helpful. (School information pack)
Your account has been debited as above. (Postal receipt)
Are you getting turned down time and time again for the job of your dreams because you just don't have the right letters after your name? (Spam e-mail)
Try to fill your bag and leave it visible of the road. We will come, rain or shine, between 8.00 am and late. (Charity appeal for unwanted clothes)

A question of context
Real-life letter-writing practice

Think about it

Different contexts involve different types of text. Some situations in life still call for a letter (and others an e-mail). You can help your class to practise letter-writing skills – often tested in examinations, too – by exploring *real* scenarios, and perhaps being '*really*' useful at the same time.

Get it ready

You need to be alert for spotting contexts which come up in class and which can be used for practice of this sort.

An example might be a real-life complaint or need for information, or a query connected with school life. Ask the person who has mentioned it if you can use their scenario for some letter-writing practice with the class. Things like:
> Needing to complain to an airline about a cancellation
> Wanting to find out what happened to a prize promised for winning a school competition

Set it up
Say that you will be using X's real-life situation as the context for a real letter which you are going to send.

Elicit and write on the board a basic framework for a semi-formal letter, like the one below.

Let it run
- The class interview the person who has mentioned their complaint, finding out as much as possible about the background and what they want to happen as a result of sending the letter.
- In pairs, they draft a version of the letter.
- They exchange drafts with another pair, marking anything they think needs adjusting. They discuss, adjusting their own work as appropriate.

Round it off
Everyone reads out their letters. Using the best phrasing from their texts, create a composite letter on the board, highlighting further adjustments you might want to make.

Follow-up

In an English-speaking environment, send the letter – in English! You may even get a reply that can be read out (using e-mail can speed up the process). Otherwise, translate it into the learners' first language: translating a text the class has created in English is also a useful exercise.

> *Dear Y*
> *I'm writing to …* [reason for writing]
> [Explanation/background]
> [Request for action to be taken]
> *We look forward to hearing from you.*
> *Yours sincerely*
> *X*

Focusing on form

Focusing on learners' lives means that the language that emerges in class will be relevant to them, but there is still work to be done if both you and they are to make the most of it. This is where a focus on form comes in.

The support you provide when focusing on form will help your class to improve their accuracy, develop their fluency and extend their repertoire.

Some techniques can be used unobtrusively, as people are speaking – by echoing, you can prompt people to fine-tune their own output, while recasting involves helping your students by rephrasing their ideas in more sophisticated language.

At other times, the focus on form will be more explicit but, even then, it is better to think in terms of refining rather than correcting.

The activities here can, of course, be used on their own, but you will find that many of these techniques for focusing on form can also be used in conjunction with conversation-driven activities presented elsewhere in Teaching Unplugged. *As you explore them, you will find which are most helpful to you and to your class.*

Retrieving

A lot of useful language comes up in class, but it can be wasted if you don't write it down. Making unobtrusive notes during lessons means that you can return to this language whenever you want to focus on form.

It's a good idea to involve the class in this: writing down language as it comes up makes 'physical' the act of noticing, creates reference points for language development, and aids recall.

Refining

Refining techniques are central to unplugged teaching. They reflect an approach to language which is exploratory, not didactic: an approach in which usage, rather than being right or wrong, is more – or less – standard; more or less appropriate to context, more or less expressive. Like much of the activity in *Teaching Unplugged*, refining techniques reflect an interest in the *process* of language production, where there is something to be learned from each stage. They can be adapted to suit learners at different levels, and paired with many other activities.

Recognising

When we encounter text in our first language, we bring all our experience of *other* texts in that language. When listening, we process the unstressed syllables that – in English, at least – lie 'hidden'. When we read or listen, we recognise collocations (word partnerships), which allow us to read phrase by phrase, or 'chunk by chunk', not word by word. We quickly identify lexical sets, allowing us to make sense of unfamiliar words from context. We recognise, and follow, narrative patterns.

Drawing attention to patterns at word, phrase and narrative level will help your class to do the same – encouraging them to tackle texts outside class with more confidence.

Reworking

You and the learners should always aim to *do* something with the language that emerges in class. Simple tasks such as copying and repeating will boost recall, but you can go further by prompting people to generate vocabulary sets and collocations from emergent language. This is a shared, exploratory enterprise and there is often no single right answer. You can also help by developing practice activities of your own between lessons: home-made substitution tables are a good way to focus on elements of form that have emerged in class.

Focusing on form

Tips and techniques

1 As soon as people start to speak, they are generating the raw material for a focus on form. Get into the habit of noting down any words or phrases that you think could be useful as soon as the lesson starts.

2 You can take notes on a piece of paper, for reference later in the lesson. This works if you are sitting informally among the class. At other times, you can make notes on the board, so that everyone can see what you intend to focus on. Involve the class in note-taking, too: they cannot rely on you to do the noticing for them *outside* the classroom!

3 Good boardwork is essential, and becomes increasingly important the less you use a coursebook and the board becomes your primary shared reference point. Find a way of using the board that works for you – from the way you write to the way you organise the space. Practise writing in different sizes and even styles – you may need to develop a different 'hand' for writing on the board.

4 Small texts can generate rich language work. Remember that texts can be written or spoken, long or short – conversation is an important unplugged source of text, and capturing even a single utterance or minimal piece of dialogue in the classroom will allow you to focus on details of form.

5 Talking about language is an integral part of unplugged teaching, and a focus on form can happen at any time: between activities, or when there is a natural pause in conversation. Don't feel you have to save everything up for the end of the lesson. Focusing on form may be built into an activity from the start, or it can be something you introduce as the situation demands – for example, as a quick burst of extension work.

6 Highlight language that has been used in the day's lesson: this is very motivating, and paying close attention to details of form will build confidence in your unplugged approach.

7 There are two broad areas to look out for when highlighting learner language. One is *successful* usage (because it mirrors standard forms or because it is expressive). The other is *less successful* usage (because it uses non-standard forms, because it is unclear, or because it could be more expressive). Examples of both more and less successful usage are equally important in terms of learning opportunities: so strike a balance between the two.

8 Some of the best linguistic support you can give is non-verbal. Smile and show interest in what is being said. This will encourage the learners to experiment – and your class will soon learn to recognise a quizzical look when you want someone to try saying something differently.

9 Encourage the people in your class to buy a notebook, to write something in it every lesson, and to look it over every night.

10 Recommend that everyone buys a good learner's dictionary, and that they bring it to school every day. This includes you! Using a learner's dictionary will give you ready access to clear definitions, and will help you to see language from the learners' point of view. (There are two dictionary-based language-reinforcement activities under 'Learning from lesson to lesson', see page 79.)

Focusing on form means exploring language that has emerged in class. Key terms:

- **Recognising** – to adopt linguistic features, learners must notice them first.
- **Retrieving** – learners should be active in recording language that comes up in class.
- **Reworking** – to learn new words and phrases, people must find ways to use them.

You can draw attention to form in different ways:

- **Replaying** – repeat what people say verbatim, so *they* can spot possible changes.
- **Recasting** – repeat what people say, making changes but without further comment.
- **Refining** – make direct suggestions that will help to improve accuracy or expression.

What did I say?

Using spontaneous remarks as text

Think about it

The classroom should be like a beehive, with people collecting words to store and explore.

Get it ready

There's nothing to prepare.

Set it up

Stop yourself after saying something in class. You might have said something like: *OK – hold on – oh, this isn't going to work.*

Let it run

- You ask your students what they think you just said.
- They confer in pairs and one pair dictates their version back to you.
- After writing up on the board what they *think* you said, you write what you *remember* saying.

Round it off

Compare the two versions, and invite the students to identify the similarities and differences.

Follow-up

Repeat this from time to time, and tell people that they, too, can 'pause' the lesson at any time if they want to check what someone just said.

Variation

You can use this activity to tell a longer anecdote, which you can even note down in advance of the lesson. This might be a description of something you happened to see on the way to school, or it could relate to your experience and opinion of something connected with a coursebook topic.

Invite the learners to reconstruct what you have said, before they share anecdotes or opinions of their own.

All aboard!

Recording language as it comes up

Think about it

Because noting and 'reworking' language is so central to unplugged teaching, it is worth paying special attention to your boardwork. Asking your class for feedback will help to improve it, and will also encourage them to focus on their own note-taking.

Get it ready

Make sure you have markers in three or four colours.

Set it up

Tell your class that you always note relevant language as it comes up, but that you want to do it in ways that are most useful to them.

Brainstorm and note on the board some of the different ways in which language might be organised. For example: new words and phrases, language that caused problems, etc.

Let it run

- Working in groups, people discuss the best way to use the shared board space.
- You circulate and answer questions, as appropriate.
- Each group draws a diagram of the board that shows how they would like it to be organised.

Round it off

Display all the group diagrams. Invite everyone to look at them and choose their favourite suggestion. They should not vote for their own idea.

You base your boardwork on the 'winning' layout for a given number of lessons, and invite feedback at the end of that time.

Follow-up

Working in groups, ask people to share the ways in which they organise their own notes in class. Ask each group to report back to the class on one of the ideas that are working for them. If it turns out that few people are making notes in this way, this is a good opportunity to highlight how useful it can be! (You can also have individual feedback sessions, to ask people how they are organising their own notes in class. Encourage and make suggestions, as appropriate.)

Who, what, when

Noting down what your classmates say

Think about it

Unplugged lessons are rich in personal detail, and focusing on the 'human' context can help people to remember new words and phrases.

Get it ready

Think of something you enjoyed doing recently, and think of one key word relating to this. For example, if you went to a concert, the word might be: 'violin'.

You will need some slips of paper.

Set it up

Tell the class that you are all going to talk about something they recently enjoyed doing. Say you want them to take turns to note down *who* is talking, *what* they are talking about, and *when* they did it.

Do a test run. Ideally, stand in a circle. Explain that you are going to tell them about something *you* enjoyed doing recently, and that you want the person on your left to make notes as you do this. Write down your key word on a slip of paper, hold it up, and elicit questions from the class, using the key word as a prompt. Then ask the note-taker what they have written down.

Give everyone a slip of paper.

Let it run

- Everyone writes down a key word relating to what they did at the weekend, for example.

- In whole class, each person in turn holds up their key word and answers questions from the class about what they did. You encourage and help with language, as needed.

- The person to the left of the speaker makes notes as they are speaking. Repeat this until everyone has answered questions about what they did.

Round it off

Take in all the slips of paper and redistribute them so that everyone has the notes of someone else's record of the conversation.

People use these notes to write a brief summary of what that person said, adding to the note anything else they can remember, including any contributions made by you or the class.

Finally, everyone reads out their account of each other's weekend activities. If anything has been left out or misreported, the person in question should say so.

The lesson that was

Writing down outcomes after the event

Think about it

A conventional lesson plan outlines what language will be covered, via what means, in the lesson to come. An unplugged lesson plan (a 'post-plan') records the language that emerged, in what context, in the lesson that has just passed.

Get it ready

Divide a page into four, and decide what your four 'big' organising principles will be. They might echo the way you organise your boardwork (see *All aboard!* on page 62), but you may want to do something different. You could use areas like these:

> *New words*
> *New phrases*
> *Forms we explored*
> *Things we discussed*

Write your post-plan, but don't try to record too much. Your unplugged lesson plan should represent 'highlights' from the lesson, rather than a complete transcript. Five entries per section is a good rule of thumb.

Make copies of your plan: enough for everyone in class.

Set it up

Distribute copies of your completed plan to the class.

Let it run

- Working individually, people mark anything they have a question about.

- Working in pairs, they discuss these questions with their partner.

- Working in groups, they discuss any questions they still have.

Round it off

In whole class, discuss and answer any remaining questions.

Follow-up

Make this a regular procedure, inviting feedback on the process you are using from time to time. You can ask people to list one thing they would change about your post-plan template, and one thing they would keep the same.

Six of one

Helping learners to notice their mistakes

Think about it
Noting, highlighting and 'replaying' learner language is a core process in the unplugged classroom. It is possible to balance 'error correction' with encouragement.

Get it ready
This activity draws on the notes you have made during a conversation activity.

Set it up
Say that you are going to write up twelve examples of language that has just been used by the class. Explain that six of the examples are 'successful', and that six could be improved.

Tell them that you are not going to write who said what, as it isn't important: you have chosen the examples because they are relevant to everyone.

Write the examples on the board. Invite people to think about them, without speaking, as you write.

Let it run
- Talking in pairs or small groups, the class decide which are the successful examples, and which ones could be improved.
- They compare their ideas with another pair or group.
- Someone tells you what their group concluded, and you check if the rest of the class agree. Finally, you confirm which are which.

Round it off
Explain why you chose the successful examples. Then, as a class, discuss how the others can be improved.

Follow-up
Everyone chooses the six examples from the board that are least familiar to them (whether these are ones that needed adjusting or not) and writes a number of sentences (or a single paragraph or dialogue) that uses each one in context.

Variation
You can use examples from the learners' written work – either during class or as homework – and follow the same procedure.

One more time

Prompting people to fine-tune their output

Think about it
Simply correcting learner language often makes no impact, especially during a communicative activity when people are focused on getting their ideas across. Encouraging learners to adjust their own output will help.

Get it ready
There's nothing to get ready.

Set it up
Explain that you will raise your hand when you want the learners to try saying something differently (this may because usage is unclear, non-standard or less expressive than it could be).

Let it run
- In pairs, people share a detail from their everyday life, such as a moment when they felt happy at the weekend. You make sure each partner gets the same amount of time to speak.
- In whole class, everyone tells the rest of the class what their partner told them. When you want them to say something differently, raise your hand.
- If they can't recast for themselves, the rest of the class help, or you make your own suggestion.

Round it off
Ask people to note down any instances they recall of you prompting them when they were speaking during that lesson. Tell them to write down:

What they said in the first place;

what they said (with or without assistance) the second time

Invite people to ask you questions if they need to, and to show you their notes once they have finished.

Follow-up
These notes can be used as the basis for individual or group feedback sessions.

Variation
Use different 'zones' or phases of an activity to focus separately on different aspects of output (see *In the zone* on page 65).

In the zone

Concentrating on different aspects of output

Think about it
If you tell the class that you will be paying attention to specific aspects of their spoken output at different stages of a lesson, it will add focus to free-flowing conversation activities.

Get it ready
Decide on a language area you would like to focus on.

Set it up
Tell the class that you will be focusing on three different aspects of their output at different times during the lesson. For example:
> Grammar
> Vocabulary
> Pronunciation

Write the three 'zones' on slips of paper and jumble them up.

Let it run
- Someone picks one of the slips of paper, and you start the lesson by focusing on this aspect, explaining that any feedback you give will relate exclusively to this until it changes.

- As people speak, give feedback by echoing (repeating what someone has said), recasting (suggesting a different way to say something) or silent prompting (using a facial expression or a gesture to invite them to try again).

- After roughly a third of the available time has passed, ask someone to choose another slip of paper, and move into that zone. Then repeat, so a third of the lesson has been focused on grammar, a third on vocabulary and a third on pronunciation.

Round it off
Invite everyone to share with a partner three things they have learned about language from this activity.

Variation
You can experiment with an alternative set of zones, such as:
> Accuracy
> Fluency
> Complexity

Spot the differences

Exchanging text orally

Think about it
An activity that begins with a written text and passes through different stages of correction and redrafting provides practice in all the skills.

Get it ready
Think of some simple, brief writing task that will engage your class. Depending on their age and interests, you could use task types like these:
> *The best way to ...* cook spaghetti/kim chi, etc.
> *The reason why ...* teenagers and parents/men and women often argue, etc.

Set it up
Write a choice of writing tasks on the board.

Tell the class they will be working in groups, and that they should produce a text of 50-100 words.

Let it run
- People discuss the task they choose in their groups and write a first draft.

- They pass their draft to you. Instead of writing on their draft, you write out a new version of their text – refining form and substituting more natural words, as required.

- You hand back both versions of the text. They compare your version with their initial version, identifying and discussing any changes you have made. You circulate, answering any questions.

Round it off
In whole class, each group selects three important changes that were made to their text. You write these on the board and discuss with everyone. Why were the adjustments necessary or helpful?

Follow-up
For homework, people ask at least one person for their opinion on *The best way to ...* or *The reason why ...*, using the same subject they wrote about in class. They make a note of this and bring it to class. If they can have this conversation in English, so much the better. If not, noting it down and telling the class about it in English is also worthwhile.

Variation
If you have a small class, you can do this activity orally. Working in groups, people produce a draft text which they dictate to you. You note it down, making any changes as you go along. You then dictate your version to the group. They write it down, and look for any changes between the two versions. You then hand them back their original to help them spot the differences.

Schwa wars

Identifying sounds in spoken text

Think about it

Pattern recognition is an important element of pronunciation – the ability to notice is linked to the ability to reproduce, and English orthography doesn't always help. For example, the most common vowel sound in English is the unstressed 'schwa', but it isn't readily apparent from the written text *where* it will appear. An activity like this one will boost recognition.

Get it ready

Find a short text: a few sentences will do. Read it out aloud to yourself, and identify where the schwas are. A phonetic dictionary may useful and, if you want to, you can compare notes with a colleague.

Set it up

Elicit the 'schwa' sound by writing the phonetic symbol on a board. Practise the sound on its own, then in a word in which it features (*lesson*) and then in a phrase (*today's lesson*).

Write your text on the board, and ask the class to copy it down.

Let it run

- Working in pairs, people read the text to each other and predict where the schwas will be.

- You read out the text at a moderate but natural speed. They mark where they hear schwas.

- You read the text again, and they make a final count. Each pair marks the schwas in pen, together with the total schwa count, and hands in their text.

Round it off

Look at the texts – the pair that has correctly identified the largest number of correct schwas wins!

As their prize, they get to read the text to the class, with the schwas in place.

Variation

Instead of identifying every example of the schwa, you can ask people to listen out for high-frequency function words that are often (but not always) pronounced as a schwa: examples include *the*, *a*, *to* and *of*.

You can also use the same process to focus on other phonetic sounds.

Textplosion!

Categorising words according to function

Think about it

Analysing text doesn't have to be very complicated – and it can help people to understand the roles played by different kinds of word. Asking the class to place words in one of two categories – 'content' (*car, road, drive*, etc.) and 'function' (*the, of, and*, etc.) – is a good place to start.

Get it ready

Choose a short text. You can vary the nature and complexity of the text to suit your class, but it shouldn't be more than 25-30 words long.

'Explode' the text, by copying each word onto its own piece of paper. Prepare a full set of words for however many groups of four or five you will have in class. Try out the task yourself before the lesson, perhaps comparing notes with a colleague, and bring a copy of the full text to class.

Set it up

Divide the class into groups of four or five. Give each group a complete set of the words.

Working in groups, people try and guess what kind of text it is, from the words in front of them. Ask which words gave them clues, and then confirm what the text is and where you found it.

Explain that you want them to divide the words into two columns: *information content* and *grammatical function*.

Let it run

- In their groups, people discuss and move the words into two columns.

- Meanwhile, you divide the board into two columns, labelled *Content* and *Function*, and ask two representatives from different groups to write up the content and function words, respectively, on the board.

- Discuss this as a class: did any group assign the words differently? You move words between columns, as required. Elicit the parts of speech that appear in the different columns, using the conversation to revise this useful reference vocabulary.

Round it off

Collect in the pieces of paper and erase what is on the board.

Dictate the words that were written up, and then ask people to work in pairs to write a reconstruction of the full text.

Variation

Ask the class to group the words by part of speech, rather than the broader categories of content and function.

Scrambled ex.

Decoding a sequence of events

Think about it

If every narrative was told in chronological order, starting with the first event and ending with the last, we would only need the past simple tense (and stories would be very boring). 'Unscrambling' a narrative, by placing events in chronological order, helps learners to focus on the roles that different verb forms play in text.

Get it ready

Find a text with a strong narrative and a variety of verb forms – news stories about crime and human interest often work well. Prepare copies of the text, if you plan on distributing it.

Set it up

Explain that you want the class to place the events described in a text in chronological order – in the order in which they actually happened – which is not necessarily the order in which they appear in the text.

Depending on the length of the text, either: distribute copies of the text, write it on a board, or dictate it.

Let it run

- Working in groups, people note down each verb form, rearranging the events described in the text in chronological order. You answer any questions they may have relating to the meaning of the words, but let them decide on the order.

- One group tells you the order they have decided, and write this on the board. You discuss with the other groups, and finalise the order.

- The class rewrite the story as a full text in strict chronological order, using only the past simple.

Round it off

Compare this version with the original, discussing how the different verb forms contribute to the narrative. What is their role:

    in referring to different periods of time?
    in contributing to the structure of the story?
    in making the story more interesting?

Follow-up

Using the 'past simple only' version for reference, people reconstruct the original text – 'rescrambling' the narrative – using the full range of verb forms you have discussed.

A drop of text

Identifying lexical fields

Think about it

When we encounter unfamiliar words in a second language, we try to guess the meaning from the context. We do this by narrowing down the range of possible meanings, deducing, for example, that a word must be connected with one of the main themes of the text.

Get it ready

Find a brief news story – curious crime and human interest stories often work well.

Set it up

Read out the headline. Ask the class to guess what kind of story it will be, and to predict two or three lexical fields (or vocabulary areas) they would expect to find in the text. Write these suggestions on the board.

Write the whole text on the board – leaving some space, as you will be needing it for writing up columns of vocabulary

Let it run

- Working in groups, people discuss whether any *other* lexical fields do in fact emerge from the text.

- The class suggest any alternative lexical fields. You agree on these (four maximum), and write them on the board, forming columns.

- In pairs or small groups, people go through the text 'dropping' words or phrases into the categories you have agreed. Tell them to write down both words and phrases they *know* and ones they *don't know*, if they think they belong in that lexical field.

Round it off

Ask someone from each group or pair to fill in one of the columns on the board, and invite comment from people in other groups.

Discuss any words that are unfamiliar, encouraging people to deduce meaning from context.

Follow-up

Using a similar text – another crime story, for example – people look for words or phrases that recur. This will boost pattern recognition. You can also recommend that people look for similar stories for homework (see *Have you got a match?* on page 81).

Lazy phrases

Rebuilding a text using its constituent parts

Think about it

The ability to identify 'chunks' of text helps listeners and readers to decode text more easily. This is a largely unconscious process for native speakers, and giving learners ready-made chunks is a good way to prompt them to start noticing chunks in English.

Get it ready

Find a short text, perhaps a news story, about something which is reasonably familiar or relevant to your class. Asking your colleagues for *their* point of view if need be, identify the key chunks which carry the meaning of the text.

Write each chunk on a different piece of paper, and make several sets – enough for groups of three or four to have their own full set. (It will help if you transcribe all the punctuation marks and capital letters.)

Set it up

Divide the class into groups of three or four, and give each group a complete set of chunks.

Explain that they have practically all the phrases they need to make a complete text, but that these phrases were too lazy to get themselves organised – and they want the class to do their work for them.

Let it run

- Each group tries to reconstruct the text, using the chunks and adding any other words they need to connect them.

- You collect the texts and put them up on the wall. Everyone circulates and looks at each other's reconstructed texts, without saying anything.

- People get back together in their groups with their own texts and make any changes, based on what they have seen.

Round it off

Ask one of the groups to dictate their text to you. Write it on the board, discuss, and agree a final version. Provided it makes sense and is coherent, it doesn't need to match the original exactly.

Follow-up

Find an alternative version of the same text (also see *Echoes* on page 56) and ask the class to identify the constituent chunks in that version.

Concord dancing

Exploring how words combine

Think about it

A concordance lists all the occurrences of a word in a given context (this word is called the 'node'), together with the words around it, allowing us to see how words typically work in phrases. Concordance examples can be read for reference (as listed in a corpus of usage), but they can also be generated in class. This activity is based on an idea by Jane Willis.

Get it ready

Using a text that has been covered in class, identify a 'node' word that appears at least four times, and list it complete with the words around it, as in the concordance below.

Set it up

Show the class what concordance lines look like, by writing your example on the board, perhaps using a different-coloured pen for the node.

Ask the class if they can detect any patterns or notice any differences. In the examples below, you could distinguish between uses where *have* is used as a main verb[1], as an auxiliary verb[2], or as part of a collocation[3].

Let it run

- Using texts you have covered, the class make their own individual concordances. They should look for words that are repeated at least four times in the text – these are likely to be 'function' words.

- You circulate and help as required, discussing the choices people have made, confirming or questioning the collocations they have identified.

- The class compare their concordances in pairs, pointing out the patterns they have identified.

Round it off

All the concordances are displayed for the class to browse. People ask each other (and you) any questions they have about particular examples.

Follow-up

Once your class are accustomed to this activity, you can set it as homework, choosing a number of words for them to identify from a shared text, or allowing them to find examples from a text of their own choice which they then bring to class.

we don't	**have**[1]	*very much money*
our lives	**have**[2]	*been very different*
we	**have**[3]	*a laugh*
he doesn't	**have**	*time to spend with his family*
I	**have**	*to work long hours*

Five old, five new

Building on what we already know

Think about it

A task that focuses explicitly on words that learners already know (as well as some they don't) builds confidence – and reflects the way we encounter language in real life.

Get it ready

Think of some occurrence in your daily life which you are happy to share. It doesn't need to be dramatic: the fact that it is *real* is what counts.

Bring an audio recorder to class – some mobile phones have one built in. Alternatively, see the less 'hi-tech' Variation below.

Set it up

Explain that you are going to recount a recent event in your life, and that as you speak you would like everyone to note down five words or phrases they *recognise*, and five that are *less familiar* – even if they aren't sure of the spelling.

Start the audio recording, and tell the class about what happened. This should only take a minute or so: speak naturally, use whatever language comes to you spontaneously, and don't worry about hesitation – it is natural and provides a realistic model.

Let it run

- Everyone shares the words and phrases they have noted with a partner. Meanwhile, you draw a line down the middle of the board; mark the *left*-hand side with a tick and the *right*-hand side with a question mark.

- People come to the board and write down the words they have noted.

- With the class, you run quickly through the familiar words, and discuss the meaning of the less familiar ones. Adjust spellings and highlight collocation, as appropriate.

Round it off

Invite the class to work in groups and use their notes to reconstruct the anecdote in writing. When they have made a first draft, play back the recording so that they can make adjustments. Then ask each group to read out their version.

Variation

You can simply dictate a short text and set the same task. Make sure you vary the text types when you repeat the activity.

New words for old ones

Paraphrasing each other

Think about it

Conversation exchanges are characterised by numerous minor rephrasings, and a task that highlights this process can help learners to follow and produce fluent conversation.

Get it ready

Have some slips of paper ready.

Set it up

Give an example of a problem you experienced recently, and how you felt about it. For example:

> My iPod stopped working and I was worried because I knew it would be expensive to fix.

Invite someone to tell a classmate about your problem, changing a word or phrase without changing the meaning (pronouns don't count!). For example, one could make any of the following changes:

> Luke's iPod <u>broke</u> and he was <u>nervous</u> because he knew it would <u>cost a lot of money</u> to <u>put right</u>.

Comment on any changes that have been made, suggesting alternatives as appropriate. The changes must sound natural in the context.

Let it run

- Everyone writes a sentence about a problem of their own, using your example, and shows it to you. You suggest any improvements and they redraft. Then collect the sentences, so people are working orally now.

- People work in groups of three: A tells B their problem. Then B tells C about A's problem, changing a word or phrase. C then 'returns' the problem to A, changing another word or phrase. See the illustration below.

- You answer any questions that arise about whether the alternatives sound natural.

Round it off

Read out the first of the 'original' sentences that you collected. Elicit and note on the board the rephrasings that were used. Repeat for everyone's sentences, commenting on the appropriacy and implications of the alternatives used.

Variation

This can be done silently, with people simply writing notes to each other that rephrase the previous note. You can also introduce a competition element by writing each completed sentence on the board in turn, seeing which pair can make the most natural-sounding changes to the sentence.

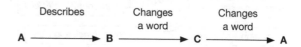

Connections and directions

Exploring links between words with a word map

Think about it

Words can be recorded and explored in the form of 'mind maps' or 'word maps'. It starts with homework for the teacher, and can be homework for the learners, once they know the process. The exploration itself is as important as the choice of the words.

Get it ready

Choose a word that you would like the class to explore further. The idea is to extend the word in as many 'directions' as possible. Try it out yourself between lessons, and bring your notes to class.

Adjectives are a good place to start – using the word *black* as the root, you can derive *white* (opposite), *dark* (synonym), *blacken* (verb derivation), *pitch black* (collocation), *blacklist* (compound noun) and *black and blue* (idiom).

Set it up

Write up your selection of words randomly on the board (for example: *black, white, dark, blacken, pitch, list, and blue*) and invite the class to connect them in any way they see fit.

Discuss their answers, and then rearrange the words into a diagram, with *black* in the middle and with the links labelled, like in the illustration below. Invite people to think of other words to add to the *black* map.

Let it run

- Working in pairs or small groups, and using dictionaries, people experiment with other productive words, such as *head, sun, world, heart*. (You can write a selection of root words on the board for people to choose from, or they can experiment with words of their own.)
- You circulate, encourage and help with language.
- Using the diagram on the board as a template, the learners draw their own mind maps.

Round it off

Each pair or group puts their mind map up on the wall, and the whole class browse each other's diagrams. You answer any questions that arise.

Follow-up

Encourage people to record and extend new vocabulary in this way for homework, and share their mind maps regularly.

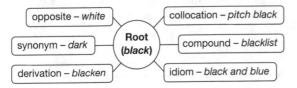

A journey in time

A verb-form workout

Think about it

Practising verb forms in isolation hardly ever seems to do much good. Why not prompt people to use several, using the same context?

Get it ready

There's nothing to prepare, but you will need a dice.

Set it up

Write this on a board: *How do you relax?*

Use gestures to invite people to ask you the question, and then say how you relax, for example by listening to music, swimming, etc.

Let it run

- Working in pairs or small groups, people ask each other the same question.
- When they have had time to discuss this, you write on the board and draw to their attention:
    How did you relax when you were a child/a teenager/younger?
  After a time, you write this:
    How do you think you'll relax when you're a grown-up/elderly?
  Finally, you write this:
    How would you relax if you were very rich?
- You circulate at each stage, encouraging everyone to speak and helping with language, as appropriate. Note down the different ways people speak about past, future or hypothetical time, including examples of standard and non-standard usage.

Round it off

Each group tells the rest of the class some of the things they discussed. Prompt, so they talk about past, present and future (though not necessarily in that order).

Using your notes, write on the board some examples of the different ways the class were talking about time. Distinguish between standard and non-standard usage, highlighting (and supplying) standard form as needed.

Follow-up

You can now introduce an element of surprise by using a dice. Write the following on the board, and roll the dice for random students in turn:

1 *What sort of food do you like?*
2 *What did you have for dinner yesterday?*
3 *What do you think you'll have for dinner tonight?*
4 *What would you have for dinner if could have anything you wanted?*
5 *Ask your neighbour any of the above questions.*
6 *Ask the teacher any of the above questions.*

Most politicians, few dogs

A home-made substitution table (1)

Think about it

If a form requires further work, you can create your own grammar 'exercise' by using a substitution table – highlighting a key form while leaving it to the learner to introduce meaning, giving the activity real communicative purpose. The example is derived from 'why' questions.

Get it ready

This is 'homework' for you to do between lessons. Start from a sentence that contextualises the form, put it into a simple table and remove one of the elements, as in the example.

Set it up

Write your table on the board.

Ask the class, individually, to use the table to make a question that they would really like answered. For example: *Why are most teachers women? Why do all politicians lie?*

They write their question at the top of a blank sheet of paper. You circulate and check the questions.

Let it run

- Each person passes their question to the person sitting on their right.
- They each read the question they have been given, and write an answer *at the bottom of the paper*.
- They then fold the answer over, so that it is out of sight, and hand the paper on to the next person, who does likewise. This continues until the paper returns to its original owner, who then opens out the answers, reads them, and selects the best one.

Round it off

Everyone reads out their original question to the whole class, followed by their favourite answer, before finding out who wrote that answer. Invite the class to comment. Do they agree or disagree? As people do this, note the language that emerges from the answers.

Follow-up

Everyone has to get two more answers to their question from other people before the next lesson: if they can ask English speakers, so much the better. If not, they can have the conversation in another language and translate the answers into English.

Why	are	all many	parents teachers		?
	do	most some few	politicians men/women dogs		

You've got a friend

A home-made substitution table (2)

Think about it

The need for participants to provide meaning when using a substitution table to focus on form creates communicative purpose. Again, this makes the process pro-active, roots the form in personal context, and will help with recall. The example involves relative clauses.

Get it ready

Prepare your substitution table. Experiment with suitable sentences, until you have examples that are straight-forward and natural.

Set it up

Write your table on the board.

Demonstrate the task by constructing a true sentence based on the table. In our example:

I've got a friend who collects rocks.

Invite the class to ask questions, by pausing expectantly. Answer the questions, and wait for more to emerge.

Let it run

- Everyone constructs a true sentence using the table and writes this down.
- A volunteer comes and sits at the front of the class, and reads their sentence aloud. They answer any questions that are directed at them (if they don't wish to answer a particular question, they should simply say *No*).
- You listen, encourage and help with language, as appropriate.

Round it off

Everyone writes five sentences about other people in the class, based on the information they have just been given. For example:

Nemanja's got a friend who plays the guitar.

Follow-up

Revisit the table and invite people to reconfigure it, so that it becomes a) a negative statement, and b) a question.

Variation

You can build substitution tables using different structures, making them yourself (or inviting the class to do so) in response to forms that emerge and need further practice.

I've got a	friend brother sister	who ... whose ...
I know	someone somebody a guy/girl	

Learning from lesson to lesson

Context and continuity

When you follow a coursebook, an element of continuity is built into your teaching. Even if the content is not particularly relevant to your class, you know where you've been, and you know what's coming next. There can also be a degree of reassurance from knowing that other people are using the same book: it places your class within a wider context of English language teaching and learning. So the more unplugged teaching you do, the more important it becomes to establish context and continuity within your own classes.

Referring to external sources is one way to do this. Comparing the language that emerges in your lessons with the language set out in an external syllabus will show how much is being naturally uncovered – as well as indicating where additional focus is needed, for example in an examination class.

You can also establish internal reference points, by encouraging learners to map their aims and regularly discuss with you what they (and you) feel they have achieved.

Reinforcing language, both inside and outside the classroom, can be crucial to provide continuity and to give a rhythm to the week, or to a sequence of lessons, and to ensure that the language that has emerged doesn't escape!

Referencing

By focusing on form at intervals during the lessons, you will generate a dynamic environment with plenty of opportunities for learning. Integrating *external* reference points (such as syllabus requirements) and *internal* measurements (generated by needs analysis and self-assessment) will help learners to make the most of these opportunities, building confidence in your independent approach.

Moderating

Moderating is a term used in qualitative market research, which shares roots with modern ELT in humanist psychology. Moderators elicit how people feel about products, experiences or ideas: even when stimulus is used, outcomes depend on who is there and what they say. The techniques in this section approach set topics from the *learners'* point of view (as well as topics chosen by the learners themselves), and can be used in conjunction with a coursebook.

Reinforcing

If your lessons are full of things that people want to talk about and the language that stems from this, make sure you take the opportunity to remind everyone of this shared experience.

You can do this via affectionate asides referring to things that have been shared in class, but the reminder can also take the more orthodox form of a test or quiz on past work.

Learner dictionaries can add an enjoyable competitive element, while placing the words uncovered in class in the context of a formal definition. And tests and quizzes can also be used to reinforce the benefits of a Dogme approach by highlighting the relationship between the language *uncovered* and the people and contexts that *generated* it.

Between lesson and lesson

One reason that grammar exercises are a popular choice to set for homework is that it's easy to see when they have (or haven't) been completed. But repeating what is essentially the same formula twenty times doesn't motivate weaker learners, and fails to challenge stronger ones.

Asking people to *do* something with language outside the classroom (placing words, phrases and forms in a context of their own devising; playing with short texts; extending lexis; noting language as they encounter it) will ensure that they practise actively, promoting both understanding and recall.

The effect of this, provided you help to maintain motivation by allowing enough time in your lessons to discuss what they have done, will be to help your students to take on responsibility and do things themselves. This is possibly the most valuable thing you can pass on to them: they won't be in your class forever!

Learning from lesson to lesson

Tips and techniques

1 Use the notes you make in class to create a link between lessons. Revisit the previous day's language notes at least once in every lesson, and use the end of the week as an opportunity to review all the notes from that week's lessons.

2 Refer *back* to activities you did in the last lesson, and *forward* to what you expect to do in the next lesson. Homework has a role to play here – setting homework which encourages people to use the language they have explored in class, and making time to go through it in the next lesson, will help to build continuity.

3 You can highlight the shared context emerging from your lessons in personal ways. As you are reminded of things that students have said or done, share it with the class, perhaps like this: *What about when Kim did that … ?* or *Federica said the same … .* But be tactful, especially when you don't know a class well: no-one wants to feel embarrassed twice!

4 Generating your own material and language in class day after day demands discipline as well as flexibility. As you find what activities work best, create informal 'staging posts' in the week: block out the first part of Monday's lesson for conversation about the weekend, for example. Link the first few minutes of each lesson to what happened in the lesson before. Find a regular weekly slot for activity that focuses on the news, and so on.

5 It is important not to lose control of the sheer volume of language that emerges from unplugged teaching. Try to strike a balance between activities that generate new language, and ones that explore and extend language already generated.

6 Helping your learners to map their aims can be a useful diagnostic tool. These will include improvement in areas such as vocabulary and grammar, but including *affective* measures, such as confidence and enjoyment, can also help you to unpick the areas in which they need more practice.

7 Keep a record of activities that you improvise in class. You may find it helpful to use the activity structure we have used in *Teaching Unplugged* as a template for your own ideas, or you may want to evolve your own framework.

8 Make gentle fun of yourself – or even of activities you tried in class that didn't quite come off – from time to time. Nothing is more ridiculous than watching someone whose hat has blown off pretending that it hasn't happened; when *your* hat blows off in class, a smile and a shrug of the shoulders is much the best response.

9 From a personal development perspective, make an effort to look up at least one language point that has come up in class in a good reference book after lessons. This will make you more confident about managing emergent language.

10 Look for ways to compare notes with like-minded teachers: this will help to place not just your lessons, but also your own professional development, in a wider context. You can look further than your own school – the internet makes it easy to exchange ideas and keep in touch.

Take a look at the Dogme site:
http://groups.yahoo.com/group/dogme/

From lesson to lesson you should make connections at a number of levels. Key terms:

- **Map** learner needs and aims together, and relate these to what happens in class.
- **Chart** your course, by recording the language generated in class, adding to this as you go along.
- **Refer** this language to learner aims, but also to external sources like a coursebook or syllabus.

Make the most of what you all achieve together:

- **Remind** people what they have talked about, both in conversation and via quizzes.
- **Revisit** language that has emerged in previous lessons, and do new things with it.
- **Explore** language inside the classroom, but also *outside* the classroom, in short bursts of activity.

73

Circular syllabus

Mapping language against an external syllabus

Think about it

A perfect syllabus would adapt to your needs, reflecting the order in which the class uncover language and revealing what remains to be explored. You can create something like this by cutting up a linear syllabus, rearranging the items at random and using it as a shared reference point.

Get it ready

Take a coursebook (the one you are using in class, or one designed for a class like yours) and identify the syllabus (this may simply be labelled 'Contents').

Copy the 'main language' or 'grammar' items from each unit onto individual pieces of paper.

Set it up

Distribute the pieces round the class. Depending on your class size, there may be one per person, or one per pair/small group, etc.

Draw a large circle on the board.

Let it run

- People talk about the item they have been given in pairs or groups, answering the following questions:
    Are they familiar with it?
    Do they use it often?
    Can they use it with confidence?

- People in turn tell the class about their item they and how they feel about it.

- In no particular order, they stick their items to the board, so that the deconstructed syllabus elements gradually form a circle as in the illustration below.

Round it off

Identify any areas that people feel need more attention, and discuss their relevance to their needs as learners (and, where relevant, as examination candidates).

Note down your circular syllabus. Make a larger copy of this in your own time, and bring it to other lessons and use it as a shared reference point.

Follow-up

Display your copy in class, and refer what emerges in each lesson to the items on the circle, by highlighting what is uncovered naturally from lesson to lesson. What is not naturally uncovered in this way will also be revealed.

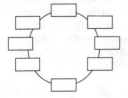

Charting your course

Keeping a record of a sequence of lessons

Think about it

By recording outputs from a number of lessons on one sheet, you can chart your course as it unfolds. This can be a valuable reference point, not just for your class but also for colleagues or those responsible for the scholl syllabuses.

Get it ready

Devise a single-page chart that organises language output from the week's lessons into different categories. You can choose these categories yourself, or (as in *All aboard!* on page 62) with the help of the class. You might group output by language area – grammar, vocabulary, pronunciation, and so on – or using headings, such as *new language, language we revised*, etc.

By hand, or in a PC document, record key outputs from each lesson on a single chart. Make a final 'clean draft', for copying and distributing at the end of the week.

Set it up

Give everyone a copy of the chart.

Let it run

- Working alone first, people look at the chart and mark *one* of each of the following:
    A favourite – some language I like
    A challenge – some language that is hard for me
    A question – something I would like to find out more about

- They share their annotations with a partner.

- You draw a large pie-chart, with three slices like the one below, on the board. Stand at the back of the class as people write up their favourites, challenges and questions on the chart. Discuss the *favourites* and *challenges* in whole class, finding out why people like a word or phrase, or find it difficult.

Round it off

Help with as many of the *questions* as you can, and make notes of any you want to research further for the next lesson – make sure you *do* come back to the class on it.

Follow-up

For homework, ask people to write some sentences, making use three of the words and phrases they like, and three of the words and phrases that are hard for them for discussion.

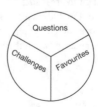

Charting your aims

Mapping learner aims and achievements

Think about it

A coursebook or examination syllabus provides a set of ready-made aims, but individual plans make a worthwhile alternative – and can be used to supplement external targets. Including affective areas, such as confidence and enjoyment, can help.

Get it ready

Think of your own use of a second or other language. In which areas are you strong? In which would you like to improve? Fill in the chart below (this kind of chart is sometimes called a 'radar' chart), and bring it to class.

Set it up

Display the chart *you* made and explain it to the class.

Let it run

- Using your own chart as a model, everyone makes their own radar chart for English.
- You circulate as they do this, asking people about the way their chart is developing. Encourage everyone to mark every area on their radar.
- People choose three areas where they would most like to improve, and share this choice with a partner.

Round it off

Have a whole-class feedback session. Ask people which areas they identified for improvement, and talk about each one as it arises, pointing out how they are being (and can be) addressed in class.

Divide the class into five groups, and give each a piece of paper. Ask each group to note down their suggestions on how to improve in one of the five areas. Then ask them to pass their notes on to the next pair or group, who should add further suggestions of their own.

Put the notes up on the wall, and invite everyone to browse them. After the lesson, you collect them and write them up in a report for the whole class.

Follow-up

If you can, hold individual feedback sessions, using the chart as a prompt. After some time, invite everyone to return to their charts, marking the progress they have made. Discuss.

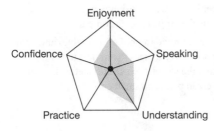

Example
High on understanding: low on practice

Result
Low on speaking: low on confidence

English from day to day

Framing the contexts of use

Think about it

The Common European Framework of Reference for Languages (CEF) is a document designed to provide a common basis for modern language teaching in Europe. It is as exhaustive as its name suggests, and it contains riches for the unplugged teacher: freely available online, it is aimed not only at people planning courses, but also at learners planning their own learning. Why not explore it?

Get it ready

Using as a prompt the 'External context of use' grid on page 48 of the CEF, note down the contexts in which you use a second or other language.

Print out pages 48 and 49 of the CEF, enough for everyone to have their copy.

Set it up

Give everyone a copy of the grid.

Ask them to mark the contexts that are relevant to *their* English use. Prompt them to include listening and speaking, reading and writing, and invite them to add any contexts they have thought of that are *not* included.

Let it run

- People mark their grids. You answer any vocabulary questions that arise.
- People compare their grids in pairs, looking for similarities or differences.
- Everyone puts their grid up on the wall, and people browse them.

Round it off

Working in whole class, discuss which contexts – current and future – are relevant to most people.

As you talk, mark these on your own blank copy of the grid, which becomes your 'Common Class Framework'.

Follow-up

Use this communal grid as a reference point for language that emerges in future lessons, marking and adding contexts as they emerge.

Use the plan to help you initiate activities that address relevant areas, if these are not being 'uncovered' naturally in class.

Encourage people to make and keep notes on their individual grids. These can also be used in one-to-one feedback sessions.

***The Common European Framework
of Reference for Languages***
http://www.coe.int/T/DG4/Linguistic/Source/
Framework_EN.pdf

Mental mapping
Brainstorming response to a given topic

Think about it

If you regularly teach topics dictated by your coursebook or the syllabus, you can start by exploring people's immediate associations – this generates discussion and relevant vocabulary before you even open the book. Drawing out and developing responses, rather than teaching pre-planned input, is a key moderating technique.

Get ready

Choose a topic: it might be the next unit in the book you are using, or you can invite your class to choose from a shortlist.

Set it up

Announce the chosen topic – a single word or phrase written on the board should be enough – and invite the class to tell you what they immediately associate with this subject.

Let it run

- The class call out their associations. You act as 'scribe', writing up on the board all the associations so that everyone can see them as you go along.

- Don't question individual choices, but do probe for a wider range of response. If, for example, all the ideas are positive, ask if anyone has any negative thoughts to add. If all the associations are concrete and literal, ask if anyone has in mind feelings or more personal associations.

- Working in small groups, people organise the words written on the board into categories of their choice.

Round it off

Invite each group to explain to the rest of the class the categories they have chosen, and why.

Variation

Write the topic on the board and ask people to work in pairs, preparing a number of questions for other people about the topic. They then write up the answers as an article about it.

Collage board
Making a visual representation of a topic

Think about it

Starting topic-based work with a visual stimulus is another way to approach it from the learners' point of view. The visual focus can help to involve less fluent speakers from the start.

Get it ready

You'll need some magazines, some large pieces of cardboard, perhaps scissors, and some glue. The magazines can be in English or in any other language. Why not ask colleagues to bring in any magazines they're planning to throw out or recycle?

Set it up

Choose a topic. This can be the next topic in the coursebook, or you can give the class a shortlist of possible subjects and ask them to choose. Divide the class into groups, and give each group some magazines. Explain that you want them to find images that represent how they feel about the topic.

Set a time limit, but don't stick to it too rigidly if people need more time.

Let it run

- People work in their groups, tearing out images and sticking them onto the cardboard to make a collage. They should tell each other *why* they have selected any image they chose.

- You circulate, taking an equal interest in each group's work and supplying any language they are reaching for as you listen.

- When the time is up, each group displays their board at the front of the class.

Round it off

Invite each group to talk the others through their collage board, explaining why they have chosen their images, and answering any questions that come up – you can ask one or two of your own questions to encourage the others.

Variation

Depending on who you are teaching, divide the class by gender or age-group so that male and female learners, or older and younger learners, are working on different image boards – this can make for interesting comparisons.

Alternatively, you can provide a pool of magazines and invite individuals to choose three images that reflect how they feel about the weekend, the world, their country, etc. They can then compare these in pairs and small groups.

Card sort

Ordering and organising words and ideas

Think about it

A card sort can be used as a testing mechanism, where people organise items into the 'correct' categories. But you can also invite people to devise the categories themselves. This is a good way of adding a learner-directed element to vocabulary work, and will also prompt discussion.

Get it ready

Make a set of fifteen or so words on separate cards, for example of fruit and vegetables.

Make more than one identical set, depending on your class size.

Set it up

Divide the class into groups of six to eight people. Give an identical set of cards to each group and invite them to organise them into categories. Tell them that *they* must decide what categories to use: there is no right or wrong answer. Set a time limit.

Let it run

- Working in groups, people arrange the cards into the categories of their choice, arranging them on a table or on the floor.
- You circulate, asking about the categories they have chosen and helping with language, as appropriate.
- When they have finished, and the cards are organised into sets, each group of learners sends a representative to each of the other groups, to see how they have organised their cards. They then return and report back on what the others have done.

Round it off

In whole class, discuss the different categorisations that were used and the language that emerges from this.

For example, some people may have organised the fruit and vegetables by colour, some by taste, some by preference, and so on. Each will generate its own lexical set, which can be refined and developed at this rounding-off stage.

Variation

You can choose topics of your own, or match the activity to ones that come up during the course. For example:

> Countries in the world/areas within a city
> TV programmes
> Hobbies/activities
> Types of drink
> Shops in the high street

Celebrity sort

Sharing opinions about famous people

Think about it

People know what and who they are interested in – all they need is the opportunity to tell you. A celebrity card sort, using images they choose from local media or the internet, allows them to tell you who interests them, their feelings about them, and the place they occupy in their world view.

Get it ready

A couple of days before you want to do this activity, ask everyone to bring in two pictures of famous people – one they like, and one they dislike or are indifferent to.

Collect the pictures.

Set it up

Mix up the pictures, put the class into groups and give each group a set. Tell them to lay out these pictures on the floor, using categories of their choice. (The different things people are famous for, different levels of popularity, etc. Don't prompt unless they are stuck, or choose categories which are too simple to be interesting.)

Set a time limit, and play some music so they can't hear the other groups' conversations.

Let it run

- People discuss the task and start sorting. You circulate, helping out with essential language and advising. Make notes of the language.
- When they have finished, everyone walks round the room, looking at the different groupings and trying to guess what the categories are.
- Each group writes down what they think these categories are, then checks. Were they right?

Round it off

Elicit from each group their categories, and note these on the *left*-hand side of the board.

On the *right* side of the board, write examples of the language you noted as the groups were talking. Together, match the words on the right to the categories on the left.

Finally, explore ways of extending the language – if a set of words for describing how we feel about people has emerged, elicit and suggest ways of adding to it.

Follow-up

Tell the students they are going to a party with a group of these celebrities. They decide which group would they most/least like to go with, and why.

Variation

The students find celebrities for *you* to sort in class. Ask them questions. They will enjoy watching you perform, and answering your questions will provide rich language practice.

Moving in space

Allowing learners to set the agenda

Think about it

Asking people what they want to talk about is a good principle, but the question can benefit from some structure. 'Open Space Technology' is a humanistic approach to problem-solving in large organisations, and can be adapted for the classroom.

Get it ready

You need to have a space (or spaces) big enough for three groups of people to gather. The number of people in each group will depend partly on your class size, and partly on how many people choose to join the three different conversations that will be going on at any given time.

Set it up

Draw a grid identifying three spaces, as in the first grid below (the spaces can be different parts of the room, if it is big enough, or adjacent spaces outside, if these are available).

When everyone has arrived, welcome them and explain that they are going to take part in a special conversation class in which *they* decide the topics for conversation. (You can leave the topics completely open, or you can suggest a theme, if you think this will help to get people started – something like: *Ways to have fun in this town*, or even *Ways to improve your English*.)

Explain that anyone who has an idea for a conversation topic should write it in one of the spaces in the grid.

People who nominate topics have to stay in that space for the whole session; other people can move from conversation to conversation, depending on how interested they are.

Let it run

- Anyone who has an idea for a conversation topic, writes it in one of the spaces in the grid. It's important not to hurry this. Write in your own suggestion to get things going, if need be.

- Everyone who has not nominated a conversation then signs up for the topic that interests them most by writing their name in the relevant space on the grid. The grid now looks something like the second example below.

- The session begins. Everyone goes to the space they have chosen. The person who 'nominated' the session stays there; other people move around when they want to.

- You circulate, spending roughly equal amounts of time in each conversation.

Round it off

People report back in whole class.

Start by asking the people who nominated the subjects what they talked about: Did people agree or disagree? Did they find out anything new? Ask for more comment from the people who took part.

Finally, elicit and agree three bullet points that summarise the discussion in each space, in each session.

Follow-up

Everyone writes a paragraph about the most interesting thing they heard or discussed during the lesson.

Variation

If your class is smaller than 12, you might want to consider getting together with another class to do this activity. The additional stimulus of a new set of people to talk to can be a real bonus.

Ways to improve your English		
Space 1	Space 2	Space 3

Ways to improve your English		
Space 1	Space 2	Space 3
Meeting people	*Watching films*	*Using chatrooms*
Student 1, Student 5, Student 7, Student 8	Student 2, Student 3, Student 9, Student 11, Student 12	Student 4, Student 6, Student 10

Guess the word

Starting from the definition

Think about it

It's important to have learner's dictionaries in class, and even more important to use them *regularly*. An entertaining game will highlight the value of its straight-forward definitions.

Get it ready

Invite people to look back over their notes from recent lessons for homework. Look back at your own notes, and choose some words that you would like to revise.

If you don't already do it, bring a learner's dictionary into class.

Set it up

Divide the class into two or more groups. Explain that they are going to compete as teams, and that when you read out the definition of a word, the team to guess the word correctly first wins a point.

The teams can confer as you read out the definition, and must hit the table before they answer.

If they give a wrong answer, or fail to hit the table before answering, they lose their chance and the next team answers. If *they* guess incorrectly, the next team (or the first, if there are only two teams) gets another go, and so on. If no-one can guess the word, *you* get a point.

Let it run

- You open the dictionary and, one by one, find the words you have chosen. Don't say what the word is!
- You read out the definition, saying 'blank' whenever the given word features in the definition. The teams try to guess the word and you award a point, as outlined above.
- After each turn, you write the word on the board.

Round it off

When the game is finished, tell the class to work in groups.

Divide up the words on the board so that each group has an equal number. Tell them they now have to write definitions for the words *themselves*.

Share the definitions, compare them with the originals in the dictionary, and discuss.

Follow-up

Each team uses a learner's dictionary to test *you*, by reading out a definition as above. If *you* don't guess the word, *they* get a point.

Variation

You open the dictionary at random and scan the page for a word that you think your class has a fair chance of guessing, from your work in previous lessons.

Guess the definition

Starting from the word

Think about it

A good learner's dictionary makes a great shared resource as you advance through a course. Don't be afraid to refer to it yourself – this is a good way to show how useful it is.

Get it ready

Make a selection of words that have come up in recent lessons: nouns, verbs and adjectives work best. If you don't already do so, bring a learner's dictionary into class.

Set it up

Read out a definition for a familiar noun such as *teacher*, replacing the key word with *blank*.

Ask the class to guess the word. Discuss the language used in the definition. For example:

Someone who ... , etc.
Something used for ... , etc.

Repeat, using a different noun.

Let it run

Read out the first word from your selection.

- Working in groups, people collaborate on a definition that they think will be as close as possible to the definition in the dictionary.
- You find the entry for that word in the dictionary. The groups read out their definitions, and you award a point to the definition which you think is closest to the one in the dictionary. (This is an approximate process and needs to be conducted in a good-humoured way; if two or more definitions are equally close, award no points to anyone!)
- Read out the dictionary definition and answer any questions.

Round it off

The group with the most points at the end wins.

Follow-up

Still working in their groups, the class open their dictionaries and test *you*, by choosing a word. When you give a definition, they must decide whether or not to give *you* a point.

A test of us

Linking revision to the people in the room

Think about it
Our memory of a new word is often closely linked to the context in which we encountered it. Unplugged lessons are rich in this sort of personal context, and you can make the most of this in an enjoyable revision game.

Get it ready
Encourage people to look over their lesson notes as the week goes by. Remind them to do this after every lesson, and say there will be a quiz at the end of the week. Have your own notes ready.

Set it up
In the last lesson of the week, or equivalent, tell people they are going to contribute to a quiz on that week's lessons by asking the questions themselves. But instead of questions explicitly about *language* points, they will be asking questions about each other's week, based on what has been shared in class.

Let it run
- In groups, people write five quiz questions based on events involving members of the class that have been shared that week. For example:
  Why did Federica get upset with her landlady?
- They show these questions to you and you suggest any improvements, as appropriate.
- Meanwhile, you write some questions of your own.

Round it off
Each group asks the rest of the class their questions.

Variation
Instead of questions for each other, tell the class to devise questions for *you*. Give them ten minutes for this and leave the room while they are preparing the quiz.

Alternatively, the class write questions that are directly about *language*. You can encourage them to use 'testing' types they will encounter in examinations, such as gapped sentences and multiple-choice questions.

Kim's table

Using a table for memorization work

Think about it
If there's a form that needs extra practice, using a memorisation task can help. Why not use *words*, instead of the objects that traditionally form the memory test in 'Kim's game'?

Get it ready
Generate a number of examples of a form that the class have uncovered during their lessons, and write these on a large sheet of paper in table form. See the example below.

Set it up
Present the table by sticking the poster to the board, and ask the class to study it silently for about a minute.

Remove the table.

Let it run
- People write down as many grammatically correct sentences as they can remember.
- They check them in pairs.
- Put up the poster again, so they can check how many sentences they remembered correctly.

Round it off
Ask them to write true sentences, using the table, about themselves.

Variation
Use sentences that the class have generated for themselves using a substitution table, as in *You've got a friend* under 'Focusing on form'. Write them down, make them into a poster as above, and use the same procedure.

Jack Jenny The boss My mum Our teacher	is was	wearing carrying	(a)	black brown striped checked new second-hand	sweater. suit. shoes. jeans. trainers. umbrella. briefcase. handbag.

Have you got a minute?

Doodling with words

Think about it
Adult learners often struggle to find the time for homework, but even the busiest people have some time to kill. They can try this activity any time, anywhere, provided they have pen and paper and a little English to work with.

Get it ready
Find a short English language text from some readily accessible source: a free newspaper, an advertisement, or a printout from a website – you can always use part of a longer text. Think about the text yourself, answering the questions that you are going to ask your class to answer.

Set it up
Write the text up on the board.

Tell the class they are going to work in pairs or in groups and complete some tasks.

Let it run
- First, they mark any words *they aren't familiar with*. Discuss these as a class, inviting people to guess meaning from context, and helping as appropriate.
- Next, they find as many *collocations* as they can within the text (pairs or sets of words that are typically used together: examples from 'Think about it' above would include *adult learners*, *find the time*, *time to kill*, *pen and paper*). Discuss these, confirming which phrases are working as collocations.
- Finally, they find as many *synonyms* as they can for words or phrases in the text. Discuss.
- At each stage, you annotate the text on the board: marking unfamiliar words, circling collocations and writing up synonyms. Once they have finished, you can point out anything useful they may have missed.

Round it off
Ask everyone to find a text after school, however short, and to follow at least *one* of the three procedures above. Tell them to write directly onto the text and to bring it to the next class.

Follow-up
In the next lesson, people share the 'back-of-the-envelope' notes they have made with the class. If you think it might be useful, set aside some time for exploring these individually with each person.

Variation
People can work in three groups, with one group looking up unfamiliar words, one finding collocations, and one finding synonyms.

Have you got a match?

Looking out for language

Think about it
People often naturally connect what they have explored in class with language that they encounter outside school, but some prompting can help to make this a habit.

Get it ready
There's nothing to prepare.

Set it up
Using the notes you have taken during a lesson, list some words and phrases on the board. Make a copy of this list.

Tell the class you want them to 'match' as many of these words and phrases as possible to situations they encounter between now and the next lesson. This may be a situation in which they read, hear or use the same word or phrase, or one to which it is relevant in their own language.

Tell them to make a note of where they found their match.

Let it run
- Divide the class into pairs, and ask each pair to choose two words or phrases they would like to try and 'match'. (There may be duplication with other pairs; this doesn't matter, and can make it more interesting at the feedback stage.) Choose two words yourself – you can do this homework, too!

Between lessons
- Everyone keeps an eye out (or an ear open) for a match involving their word or phrase.

In the next lesson
- The pairs reconvene and tell each other if they've got any matches – and if so, *when*, *where* and in *what context*.

Round it off
Share the findings as a class.

Put the list of words up on the board, ask people to tick the ones they found and you answer any questions that arise.

Variation
Instead of inviting people to choose which words they want to try to match, you distribute the words at random.

Doing, thinking, feeling
Keeping a diary

Think about it
Keeping a diary comes naturally to some people, but it can help others if you suggest a framework.

Get it ready
Write a brief 'diary entry' between lessons – the weekend is often a good time to do this. Note something you *did*, something you *thought about* and something you *felt*. These things can relate to the same time or to different occasions, but do note the time and date.

Set it up
Write the words *Doing*, *Thinking* and *Feeling* on the board.

Read out your diary entry, answering any questions that arise.

Ask someone to 'play back' the notes you made about these three things orally.

Let it run
- Everyone writes a similar entry about their own weekend, for example, marking with a question mark any words or phrases they are unsure about.

- They show these entries to you. You give feedback first on the language they have marked with a question mark, and then suggest any other improvements that could be made.

- People share their diary entries in pairs.

Round it off
Everyone tells the class something about their partner's weekend.

Follow-up
Between classes: Ask everyone to do the same in their own time during the next weekend. In addition to noting an action, a thought and a feeling, remind them to include any words or phrases that have emerged in class and which fit the context.

Next time: After making sure that people are happy to share their entries with the class, read out some or all of everyone's entries in turn.

Ask questions about what they have described, and highlight:
anything that is well expressed
any use they have made of language that emerged in class

Don't worry if not everyone has done this. Prompt the class every week, to remind those that don't, and keep encouraging those that do.

Honey bees
Collecting language

Think about it
Noting language shouldn't stop at the classroom door – why not keep it going between lessons by making what the learners collect from their various sources a fundamental part of the next lesson?

Get it ready
Tell the class that the next lesson will be based on language they collect outside the classroom: words, phrases, snippets of conversation.

Brainstorm the ways in which they can do this, such as: making a mental note, scribbling something down, or even using a text function on their mobile phones.

Brainstorm the places they might find some language: a poster, overhearing a conversation (between native or non-native speakers of English). Even in non-English speaking environments, there may be access to books or CDs, to satellite TV stations or websites (also see the Variation below).

Set it up
In the next lesson, ask everyone to get their notes ready.

Let it run
- In whole class, you look at each piece of language that has been collected in turn. Ask people where they found it, and why it caught their attention.

- You ask if other people have come across the same language, in the same or different contexts. Invite comments or questions about the usage, and answer these as appropriate.

- Everyone imagines 'returning' their piece of language to the environment in which they found it, and writes a short text that places it back in context. For example: by writing more text from the poster, by writing the next line in a dialogue, and so on.

Round it off
Read out the texts and dialogues, and discuss.

Follow-up
Making this a regular lesson activity will help to make 'language collecting' a habit.

Variation
In an environment where it is really hard for people to find English language sources, tell them to collect L1 examples which they would like to be able to use in English.

C

Teaching Unplugged has so far provided activities that are deliberately open in their potential application – they are designed to come to life in class, and that life will depend on the people you are teaching. We now focus on those people, and on the ways in which Dogme can be applied in different teaching environments.

Since we started our e-group (http://groups.yahoo.com/group/dogme/), teachers have been asking each other questions about the suitability of teaching unplugged for different teaching contexts, and even for their own skills.

Unplugged applications

Very often these questions have been answered simply and affirmatively by the teaching experience of those people taking part in the debate.

Do you have to be a native speaker of English to teach this way? Our group members think not. Can you teach this way with children? Some of the most passionate 'dogmetics' already do. Can you teach people who need English for business? Again, the answer is yes.

Working people bring to class their immediate language experience, allowing you to help them shape their language to their needs. Is it possible to teach over an extended period, perhaps a term or a full year, and even organise a whole school around a Dogme philosophy? The authors of *Teaching Unplugged* think so.

Of course, there are specialised areas in which Dogme techniques need to be blended with a syllabus. Examination classes are one example and, if you are teaching English for Aviation, it would be essential to cover key areas of operational language. Even the authors would not feel comfortable waiting for language to emerge at 20,000 feet!

Unplugged indications

This part of *Teaching Unplugged*, then, addresses some of the 'frequently asked questions' about where and how Dogme may be applied – the issues involved and their implications.

We do not pretend to have all the answers, but we hope to indicate how you can confidently explore unplugged teaching where *you* are, and to find the answers *yourself*.

Teaching as a non-native speaker

Everyone, at some point in their teaching career, has experienced a breakthrough moment. For many of us this comes when a lesson takes off in an interesting way: a day when the lesson plan gets left far behind and people express themselves freely.

Some critics of the Dogme approach have suggested that only native-speaker teachers can feel fully comfortable in this unplanned teaching mode, but this has not been the authors' experience.

From talking to native- and non-native-speaker teachers about Dogme, we know that both can relish these moments of freedom. One teacher we met, a non-native speaker, recalls that in Romania there was always a delay of a month or so before the coursebooks arrived at the start of the new school year. She remembers it as being the best time of the year: 'We could do anything we liked!'. Her experience has been echoed by non-native-speaker teachers around the world.

Issues

A Dogme approach can sound high risk, involving snap decisions and an intuitive feel for both accuracy and appropriacy – the kinds of skills often associated with (experienced) native-speaker teachers.

Even teachers who are intrigued by the 'lightness' of such an approach can worry that such lightness might be unbearable – or, at least, hard to sustain. Lessons that emerge out of the conversation between the people in the room, they often argue, are just too unpredictable.

Meanwhile, the coursebook, the syllabus and supplementary materials can all appear to offer a bulwark against the threat of chaos: of a lesson spinning out of control, or the loss of face and authority on the part of the teacher. The marketing activities of the major publishing houses would seem to reinforce this – all those sponsored workshops publicising 'essential' resources must mean something, mustn't they?

Implications

The suggestion that non-native teachers are somehow deficient or disadvantaged reflects the very mindset that Dogme seeks to subvert: namely, the idea that language teaching is about the transmission of perfect models of expression.

The Dogme argument is that language teaching is about exploring and extending the learner's existing language capability. The teacher's role is to scaffold, or support, the learner's ability: not by providing native-like models, but by nudging it towards greater intelligibility and fluency.

Teaching is less about being a subject specialist than being a good communicator and a good motivator. Much more important than a teacher's competence in the targeted skill is that they have the very human capacity *to manage a group* and *to get people talking*. These are social skills – not linguistic ones. They are the kinds of skills that are valued in any context where interaction and communication are key – board meetings; counselling; dinner parties; sports coaching, and so on.

Another key attribute for language teachers – and one that can take years for native speakers to acquire – is developing an ability to see the target language through the learners' eyes. If you have been through the same journey as your class, this can be easier – especially if you speak the same first language as your learners and can reliably identify interference.

Ultimately, however, this is no more a specifically 'native speaker' issue than the social skills outlined above. What is critical is learning to approach each lesson as a shared experience of discovery: to re-learn language and, by implication, one's way of teaching it, through the experience of the learners.

Indications

- Start small – cultivate Dogme 'moments' in your classes, as opposed to whole Dogme lessons.
- Share your own language learning experiences with the learners, including tips and short-cuts you learned yourself.
- If you (or your learners!) would like the comfort and security of a book, substitute the coursebook for something else, such as a student grammar – which you can dip into from time to time – or a graded reader. A teacher we know got her class to subscribe to a magazine, and that became their coursebook.
- Use activities which can be personalised, but whose content you can control and whose outcomes are fairly predictable. One example is 'dictogloss' – you tell the learners a short anecdote about yourself or about a friend (controlled input), and then, working in groups, they reconstruct it from memory. Then they recall similar events in their own lives and tell each other (fairly predictable output).
- Exploit class bilingualism by using techniques involving translation, such as Community Language Learning.
- Take the 'weight off your feet' by encouraging peer teaching, individual presentations and show-and-tell activities.
- Take advantage of any opportunities to bring guests into the classroom, including both native- and non-native speakers. If your non-native-speaker guest speaks some English, so much the better – but if not, then conducting an interview in the learners' first language before translating questions and answers into English will still be a worthwhile task with manageable outcomes.

In short ...

It is worth keeping the big picture of English language use in mind: interaction in English between non-native speakers is becoming the norm worldwide. If English ever 'belonged' to native speakers, that time is fading fast. The British author, David Graddol, has written extensively on this: his latest book, *English Next*, is even sub-titled 'Why global English may mean the end of English as a foreign language'.

Later in the book[1] he sounds a more cautious note, suggesting that 'the ideas and practices associated with teaching *English as a Foreign Language* will remain significant factors for some time to come', but predicting that 'the declining reverence of "native speakers" as the gold standard for English' will be one of the features of a new paradigm for global language use.

Teaching in this new paradigm will be well-suited to an unplugged approach – which views the native-speaker/non-native-speaker distinction as incidental, even trivial.

[1] http://www.britishcouncil.org/learning-research-english-next.pdf

Teaching with a coursebook

> *No coursebook is going to be just right for your learners: in your institution, in their social context, on any given day of the year, or at any given time of day. With the best will in the world, coursebook writers and their publishers simply cannot produce texts that will match the huge range of variables in any one learning situation. (If this were the case, machines would have taken over the job of teaching decades ago!)*
>
> *A Dogme approach respects – and is nourished by – this diversity. Attempting to control the variables by using a coursebook is rather like opting for package tourism: convenient but impersonal, as much about fitting things into the itinerary – 'ticking off' the sights – as about the opportunity to experience and explore. Lessons that tap into the rich classroom ecology become voyages of discovery. An unplugged approach may not guarantee peak learning experiences, but it doesn't inhibit them, either.*

Issues

Most teachers – perhaps 99% – work in contexts where the use of a coursebook is mandated. A few lucky ones may actually have a say in which coursebook to use, but most don't. Even if a coursebook is not imposed from above, there is often the expectation – on the part of learners and their stakeholders (parents, bosses, and so on) – that the course will be structured around a core text. After all, this is how most courses in most subjects do it, don't they? Love them or hate them, coursebooks are a fact of (classroom) life.

And coursebooks are still shackled by the insistence of writers, publishers and exam boards on tying them to the traditional, one-small-step-at-a-time grammar syllabus. 'Today is Tuesday, so we're doing the present perfect continuous.' All the good intentions of the coursebook writers – and the teachers who use the coursebooks – are smothered at birth by the colossal weight of the grammar syllabus. It's hard to let language emerge naturally, if you have to do the present perfect continuous at the same time. And how can learners interact creatively, if they suspect that all the teacher is really interested in is a particular verb form? Grammar is all too often the tail that wags the dog.

Modern coursebooks are also increasingly unwieldy, with workbooks and digital add-ons becoming standard. An integrated approach to skills and syllabus work makes it hard to unpick one piece of content from the next, while each additional layer – from audio-visual to interactive content – implies and demands more technology. Even if one knows where to begin, it can be hard to know where to *stop*.

Implications

The good news is that modern coursebooks take seriously the need to motivate learners. They do this by choosing engaging topics, genuine texts and striking images, and – most importantly – by incorporating productive, creative, interactive, and often personalised, speaking activities. All these resources can be exploited by the enterprising teacher to centre the language *learning*, and language *using*, on the people in the room.

Here, therefore, is a compromise. The idea would be to use the coursebook, but selectively, even subversively, short-cutting the grammar, and foregrounding the interesting topics and interactive tasks. It does *not* mean, however, propping up the book's shortcomings by bringing in yet more material in the form of photocopied exercises or Powerpoint presentations. The aim is to exploit the activities that provide the optimal conditions for language learning, which are:

- (massive) exposure;
- attention;
- rehearsal;
- performance;
- feedback.

Whatever grammar work that is done will be based on:

- what learners notice in the exposure;
- what they need for the rehearsal;
- what is generated in the performance;
- what becomes the focus of the feedback.

Indications

- Generate interest *in* the topic and language *about* the topic of the current coursebook unit through the use of surveys, questionnaires, and your own personal anecdotes. You can use brainstorming activities to explore the associations people have with the unit topics, before you even open the book.
- Encourage learners to look for topic-related texts themselves, and to bring these to class to share with their classmates.
- Reserve the 'receptive' work in the unit – the reading and listening texts – for out-of-class time, so as to maximise classroom time for productive, interactive and collaborative activities, such as speaking and writing.
- If your coursebook syllabus includes 'communicative functions', think of ways in which you can refer these to people's own experience. Talk about this in class, then use the coursebook material to see what it *adds* to your classroom discussion, rather than the other way round.
- Personalise the more mechanical grammar and vocabulary exercises, where possible, by asking learners to convert them into true statements about themselves – or the other learners in the room.
- Draw attention to any grammar areas that emerge naturally and reference these to the coursebook syllabus, so as to demonstrate to learners (and their stakeholders, from parents to other teachers) that you are covering the grammar – by *uncovering* it.

In short ...
If the learners are engaged in a range of life-like tasks about a range of relevant topics and using or producing a range of genuine texts, they will be covering all the grammar they need. To the extent that the coursebook complements and enhances these processes, why not use it? But if you can get away with using it *less*, even if only from time to time, it is important not to feel you are short-changing your learners. Coursebooks may have become the orthodox way to *teach* a language, but in today's globalised and increasingly connected world, they are only one of the ways to *learn* a language.

Teaching young learners

The teaching of English to young learners is set to become a major focus of English language teaching in the next few decades, overtaking in hours and numbers the teaching of any other age group.

The exponential increase in EYL (English for young learners) has been accompanied by an associated increase in the production of materials targeting this sector. Much of this material is aimed at introducing English in an entertaining and multi-sensory fashion, exploiting the easy availability of video, computers and other technological aids.

But accessible materials and hi-tech delivery mechanisms may not guarantee the kind of active engagement that helps children to learn.

Issues

Underpinning the materials and technologies produced for the EYL market is the belief that, in Neil Postman's words, 'learning is a form of entertainment or, more precisely, that anything worth learning can take the form of an entertainment, and ought to'.[1] For Postman, a contemporary example of this approach was the so-called educational television show *Sesame Street*. Yet, 'as a television show, and a good one, *Sesame Street* does not encourage children to love school or anything about school. It encourages them to love television'.[2]

On the other hand, and alongside the rise in EYL, many regional educational authorities (often urged on by parents) are advocating the need for young learners' materials that assume a teaching approach more appropriate to older learners, emphasising rule-learning, memorisation and assessment. An extreme form of this view is the *hagwon*, the private colleges in Korea, where children are customarily led through a succession of mechanical drills and exercises as preparation for state examinations.

Needless to say, a Dogme approach distances itself from both the *entertainment* and the *cramming* models of young learner education.

Implications

It is generally accepted that young learners – at least those under the age of twelve or so – do not have the cognitive capacity to think of language in purely grammatical terms. Abstract language-specific concepts, like tense and modality, are opaque and difficult to grasp for them.

A language teaching approach that foregrounds, and makes explicit, formal grammar is unlikely to engage them, therefore. Rather, young learners learn by *doing* – by being involved in language-using activities where the focus is on the *functionality* of language: interacting with other language-users in order to get things done, to enter imaginary worlds, to create things, to exchange information or, quite simply, to play.

Moreover, language-using activity that is grounded in the young learners' own needs, interests, desires and dreams, is more likely to engage them than activities whose rationale is primarily the practice of pre-selected grammar items.

A Dogme approach, predicated on activity rather than grammar, and on the learners' emergent needs rather than on the assumptions of the absentee coursebook writer, would seem ideally suited to young learners. Unplugged teaching, in fact, shares many of the principles and practices of other progressive, early-learning educational movements.

Teaching young learners

The Montessori Method, for example, also foregrounds activity and the creation of a nurturing social community. Montessori schools adopt a holistic approach to the curriculum, where arts, science and language are integrated and where the child's natural curiosity is engaged. Similarly, in the Waldorf Schools, inspired by the philosophy of Rudolf Steiner, an academic approach to learning is de-emphasised. Typically, there are no textbooks at early grades: children keep their own 'lesson books' in which they record their experiences and their learning achievements.

In the same reforming spirit, Sylvia Ashton-Warner, the pioneering New Zealand primary school teacher (as we saw in Part A of *Teaching Unplugged*), abandoned the textbooks imported from Britain and based her teaching on the children's lived experiences: 'I harness the communication since I can't control it, and base my method on it.'

All these approaches share the humanistic values and the holistic approach of Dogme.

Indications

- Teach English through activities such as song, dance, arts and crafts, and drama.
- Use English both as a medium of expression and as the language of classroom organisation and negotiation.
- Provide scaffolding in the form of regularly-used, easily recognisable routines, and accompany 'classroom English' with gestures, facial expression and mime.
- Don't be afraid of repeating the same activities and revisiting the same texts: children have a greater tolerance for repetition than do adults.
- Use English as the medium to teach other curriculum subjects, such as physical education, music and science. (This is an approach increasingly favoured by many educational authorities, and is generally known as Content and Language Integrated Learning or CLIL.)
- Deal with language issues through feedback, and by recasting (that is, paraphrasing) the learners' output, but avoid overt correction on the one hand, and excessive praise on the other. Treat the second language as a natural and unproblematic alternative to the learners' mother tongue.
- Distribute scrapbooks to the learners, which they fill with their own stories, drawings, photos, and projects. This takes the place of the coursebook.
- Keep a record of the language areas that come up, so that you have evidence to show inspectors, parents, and other stakeholders that you are 'uncovering' the syllabus. And *explain* your approach, situating it in a long tradition of successful and transformative education.

In short ...

A colleague explained that the power of using a Dogme-influenced approach was in things like 'personalising, by speaking about your own life, bringing in pictures. I started off this year speaking about my pet. *My dog's name is Nikita,* etc. And later, when I showed them just a list of words that they'd copied from the blackboard, they said: "This is about Nikita". And it was. They immediately knew what it was about, so it's really powerful.' [3]

[1] Postman, N (1985) *Amusing ourselves to death* Methuen
[2] ibid.
[3] Nerina Conte in Conte, N and Thornbury, S (2003) 'Materials-free teaching' *English Teaching Professional*, 26

Teaching specialised English

Teaching specialised English – academic English; the English of business, of law or of technology, for example – is becoming a major ELT growth area in many regions. As more and more learners reach tertiary level with a solid grounding in the language – and as more and more people seek work outside their own countries – the demand to fine-tune their English for specialised, career-oriented purposes will intensify. Can this trend be accommodated within a Dogme philosophy?

Issues

In a sense, the need for specialised English – English for Special Purposes (ESP) and English for Academic Purposes (EAP) – is simply one manifestation of the need for instruction that is individualised, that targets the unique needs and learning styles of each individual learner. The notion of needs analysis – fundamental to any process of customising teaching – is also a basic Dogme principle. It would be easy to assume that, because the unplugged teacher is sensitive to learners' needs and finds ways to let these shape the lesson content, *all* the language generated in the unplugged classroom is 'specialised'.

The fact is, however, there is a real risk in a Dogme approach of allowing a conversational style to predominate, at the expense of engaging with the more formal registers associated with specialist areas such as business and law. And given that what differentiates these specialisations, or disciplines, more than anything else is the *kind of texts* they use, the Dogme teacher of ESP is faced with the challenge of how to balance the need to use texts with the philosophy of 'bare essentials'.

Implications

This challenge has a relatively simple solution: something that many teachers of ESP have already embraced, whether they espouse Dogme principles or not. Put simply, the learners provide the texts. As David R. Hall writes in describing the rationale underlying an EAP programme he co-ordinated in Thailand:

The potential for learners to participate in generating materials has long been neglected. I would suggest that students themselves are in a unique position to look for relevant resource materials. They know what their own needs and interests are. [1]

Accordingly, Hall and his colleagues developed a course model based on a repeated cycle of student presentations, feedback, and re-presentations. Each repetition of the cycle involves the learners exploring, in successively greater depth, both the content and the textual structure of their presentation.

As the course develops, and students begin to analyse published and unpublished academic discourse produced by others, both form of presentation and organisation improve markedly, and communication within the classroom, as well as outside it, becomes committed and almost totally student-dominated.

Significantly, *except at very few places … texts … are found and brought to class by the students themselves, so that the course content is generated by students, not by teachers.*

Of course, the fact that the activity cycle is constantly replenished by reference to published material assumes that the learners have access to a library or at least the internet. But this is not such a tall order nowadays. If anything, learners need guidance in how to *reduce* the amount of text that is now available to them, and guidance in how to *evaluate* it critically and *use* it judiciously.

Indications

- In class, use short texts representative of particular genres or styles, in preference to long ones, which might better be reserved for out-of-class reading. For example, use the *abstract* of an academic paper, rather than the whole paper, but subject its style, organisation, grammar and vocabulary (including collocations) to close analysis.
- Establish a system by which individuals take turns to present to the class a set of words that is relevant to the class's special subject – these could come from texts that they have found on the internet.
- Invite the learners to take turns giving presentations, which are discussed in terms of their content, organisation, and execution. For example: impromptu 'show and tell' presentations, using some item that they each have with them (the equivalent, perhaps, of a teacher's boardpen!) and that is relevant to their discipline, can first be rehearsed in pairs before presentation to the class.
- Tell the learners to bring to class texts they have found, along with questions about them that they have prepared themselves. They then exchange these in pairs, and read and answer each other's questions.
- Roleplay situations that are relevant to the learners' specialisation, for example conference chat between presentations, or explaining their company structure to a visitor. The learners can write, rehearse and perform their own roleplays, which are then subject to discussion and constructive criticism.
- Get the learners to write texts collaboratively on topics relevant to their discipline and in the appropriate style. These are then exchanged and improved by their classmates.
- Base the course curriculum around an extended, collaborative project – such as producing a short video or a conference presentation, or designing a website or an advertising campaign. You feed in the language that is needed *when* it is needed.
- Give short lectures/presentations yourself, for note taking and summarising purposes. When available, invite colleagues, friends, or local experts to do the same.

In short ...

Being a proficient user of a specialised form (or register) of English implies identifying with other members of the 'discourse community' that uses that register, and participating in their cultural practices.

Learning how to 'talk the talk' is facilitated if the classroom itself can become a 'local community of practice', generating its own texts and discourses.

As a Dogme approach foregrounds community and learner-generated content, it can be highly effective in the teaching of English that is highly specific to the learners.

[1] Hall, D R (2001) 'Materials production: theory and practice' In Hall, D R and Hewings, A (Eds) *Innovation in English Language Teaching: A reader* Routledge

Teaching one to one

From the learner, 'one to one' classes promise unmediated contact with a teacher.

This expectation can be compromised by the unnecessary use of published material, and it is dispiriting to see an expectant one-to-one learner heading for a classroom, closely followed by a teacher armed with a sheaf of photocopies.

While you may sometimes need to refer to published sources for specialist language, depending on the needs of the learner, this needn't be your starting point: as with English for Specific Purposes, your aim should be to draw out the learner's language – actual and potential – by talking, listening and developing leads from their own life.

The one-to-one class is, in fact, an excellent environment for Dogme teaching at its most distilled: encouraging someone to talk, making notes as they speak, and exploring together the language you have captured.

Issues

Teaching one to one can be tiring, whatever approach you take, and relying mainly on conversation doesn't necessarily make things easier: with no other learners to 'bounce off', and no group tasks to give you a moment to breathe, unplugged one-to-one teaching can feel quite demanding at first.

Just *how* demanding can depend on how you 'gel' with the person you are teaching. The teacher-learner relationship is inevitably more exposed than it is within a class environment and you may feel that there is no 'chemistry', or that you have little in common.

Expectations also work both ways. You might think that someone taking private lessons would spend plenty of time on their English between lessons, but not everyone can. Having the money to pay for one-to-one tuition can come at the expense of not having much free time. And whether your learner is doing two jobs to pay for individual attention, or working long hours for a company who is paying for their classes, you will need to be realistic about how much 'homework' they can do.

Implications

Just as one-to-one lessons promise the learner unmediated contact with a teacher, they offer you the opportunity for unmediated contact with a *learner*. If you think of a one-to-one lesson as a chance to find out more about your learner, this will provide a good model for your teaching: a lot of the time, you will be asking questions and listening. To effectively teach one to one, you need to engage creatively with the life of the learner.

It is important to remember that one-to-one learners have usually tried to improve their English on a number of occasions – often involving coursebooks and set topics. If they have been frustrated by this experience, they may well be open to a more responsive approach which focuses on the detail of their own daily lives and personal language needs.

Meanwhile, one-to-one learners often have quite specific aims. If you allow yourself to be driven by *their* needs arising from *their* context of use, this will help with your lesson planning.

And if the learner is too busy to do much work outside class, find alternatives to extended homework tasks: a single paragraph can yield plenty of language study. A little work each day is much better than none.

Teaching one to one

Indications

- Explain how you propose to teach: say that you will spend a lot of time talking, listening and taking notes. Show how this leads to a focus on form, by pausing after a little conversation to show what you have written down and discussing the language points that have arisen. Going over these notes calmly and constructively, at intervals, will reassure them that you are giving them all the feedback they need.

- Make a one-page summary of your notes before the next lesson. If you can type it out and e-mail it to your learner, so much the better. If you can't, just copy it out neatly and give it to them in person the next time you see them.

- In this summary, you can include a regular task, such as asking them to write three sentences using words or phrases that are new to them. Always take the time to go over these notes in class.

- Work on roleplays derived from real-life challenges – from 'small talk' with a business client to a conversation they are going to have with their landlord. Find out as much as you can about the situation, and provide some useful phrases that will help. Then act it out: you play the part of the business client, the landlord, and so on. Follow it up – did the conversation finally take place? How did it go?

- If the learner is too busy to do homework, ask them to contact you in English between lessons, sending you a short message. This could be a mini-report from work, or a note of what they have done that day. A single paragraph will provide ample stimulus for a subsequent focus on form, and you can use it for dictation exercises, for example, where you read their work back to them with some changes, before discussing the differences.

- Encourage your learner to keep a language diary. This can involve minimal input and will help to keep English on their radar between classes. You can give a framework to help them, suggesting that they note:
    - a word or phrase they recognised from class – and where they encountered it;
    - a word or phrase they didn't recognise – and where they encountered it;
    - a conversation they had in English (including online chat and e-mails) – and what it was about.

- It is natural to want to focus exclusively on the learner. To a certain extent, this is what they are paying for. But remember that there are two people in the room. Encourage them to ask *you* questions: sharing your experience is a good way to sustain conversation, and provides natural language models for the learner.

- And listen to the broader aspects of their production (are they speaking too loudly?), and watch their body language (do they tense up when they use English?).

In short …

Praise is an essential counter-balance to the 'correction impulse' that can affect learners as well as teachers – and perhaps even more so in one-to-one teaching. No one wants to spend an hour being constantly corrected and 'set right'. The learners are often anxious, so highlighting what they *are* doing right will help them to relax and make the best use of their time. One-to-one teaching is, in many respects, a luxury for the teacher, too. It enables you to explore a learner's English in ways that can be hard to devote individual time to in regular classroom environments.

Teaching exam classes

Teaching an examination class simplifies some of the questions that an unplugged approach must try to answer – there is, after all, no need to identify where an exam course is 'going' – but other questions may be raised. Any critical approach to education is, for example, bound to take a sceptical view of exams, whether viewed as a measure of achievement and potential, or in the context of their potentially limiting impact on teaching.

How, indeed, can one square the ethos of the exam – one-off, individual, result-focused – with an organic, co-constructed, process-oriented approach to learning: a Dogme appoach?

Issues

Whatever your feelings about the educational value of a particular exam, your overriding concern as a teacher must to be to help your learners pass. If a strict diet of past papers can achieve this, it would be foolish to rule it out as a short-term strategy. However, there can be diminishing returns from too much past-paper work, even in the short term. Past papers and example exercises are *testing* tools, after all, not *teaching* tools. Repetition alone will ensure familiarity with the exam format, but it is unlikely to lead to significant improvement. And repetition without improvement can be pretty depressing!

Learners can understandably be tense about exams, and may be influenced in this by the activities of their peers. If my friends are doing wall-to-wall practice papers with their teacher, they may ask, shouldn't we be doing the same?

Tension and monotony are not conducive to any sort of learning, exam preparation included. The extent to which you use unplugged techniques will depend on the format of the exam in question (multiple-choice test formats, for example, may need to be rehearsed on their own terms, although even these can be rendered more creative), but a more conversational, exploratory and hands-on approach to the exam syllabus can reap its own rewards.

Implications

Although some examinations are still built on multiple-choice answers, it is probably easier for unplugged teachers to work with today's exams – more text-based, more task-focused – than would have been the case twenty years ago. There has been a shift in this time from focusing mainly on people's ability to manipulate or identify discrete language points (although tests of this sort are included in many exams), towards a more task-based approach. Many elements of modern ESOL exams are thus compatible with – and indeed recommend – a teaching approach focused on people's lives.

If, for example, we look at the Reading and Writing paper from the University of Cambridge Preliminary English Test (PET), we find that candidates 'need to be able to read texts from signs, journals, newspapers and magazines and understand the main points'. All of these can be practised with activities of the sort outlined in Part B of *Teaching Unplugged*: writing short messages, stories or letters is also very much part of an unplugged diet. The final task type in this paper, which involves 'changing the meaning of sentences', is a more technical one – not something you would expect to do outside an exam. You will need, therefore, to use past papers to give your class practice in this sort of task, but you can provide *extra* practice by generating, and then changing, sentences derived from the learners' lives here.

Remember your basic tools – the people in the room, focusing on form – and add to them a basic 'examination kit': the syllabus (share it with your class!) and those past papers. You can do this by familiarising learners with the format of the examination, by highlighting sound exam techniques and by ensuring that they are confident using the forms, the lexis and the task types indicated in the exam syllabus.

Indications

- Start well in advance of the exam, for example by making the connection between a speaking activity, where the class bring in pictures taken from magazines or the internet to discuss, and the procedures of an oral exam paper.
- Highlight how the activity you normally undertake in class is relevant to specific papers.
- Identify task types tested in the exam (such as describing a picture or writing a semi-formal letter) and find ways to practise these tasks using real-life contexts. If someone mentions a problem they are having outside class, you can brainstorm ways to approach this, and then draft a class letter which endeavours to resolve it. The key is to elicit, teach and practise the *kind of structures* that the exam will test, but to retain the immediacy and engagement of *real content*.
- Help the class to generate their own exercises that mimic examination techniques – using the exam formats as a model. This will encourage them to consider relevant language and task types, and will also serve to demonstrate that examination papers don't drop, fully formed, from the skies: they are constructed by people to test specific things!
- An exam is a technical test, but it is also an event in people's lives; the lead-up to an exam is a narrative in itself. Explore people's feelings; talk about your own and their past experience of exams. Share examples of effective and less effective preparation. If you can build in a class social event *before* the exam, it will build relationships and boost morale. An event *after* the exam can be a celebration!

In short ...

However you feel about the way an exam is constructed or administered, it is important to look at exams in the context of people's lives. Exams can, after all, be highly motivating, and the results may have a real impact on further education and employment prospects.

Unplugged techniques not only have a role to play in preparing your class for this challenge, but they can also help to maintain engagement and enjoyment through what can be a stressful and somewhat monotonous time.

Teaching an observed lesson

On some in-service teacher-training courses, such as the Cambridge ESOL Diploma (Delta), teachers are required to teach a lesson that qualifies as 'experimental practice'. This means that the design of the lesson, or the materials or technology that it involves, or the actual methodology, are not part of their usual repertoire.

Many teachers choose to meet this challenge by 'doing a Dogme lesson'. This might appear a fairly high-risk strategy, given the relative unpredictability of an unplugged lesson. But taking risks is what teacher development is (or should be) about. And most examiners will forgive a less than perfect lesson, if the candidate is genuinely trying something different – especially if their rationale for doing so is well-grounded in an understanding of the principles involved, and in a clear commitment to the needs of the learners.

And, even if you are being assessed simply as part of your institution's internal evaluation process, adopting a Dogme approach might make your supervisors sit up and take notice!

Issues

Lesson assessment typically takes into account both the planning and the execution of the lesson. Assessors expect to be delivered a detailed lesson plan in advance, with the staging laid out neatly and sequentially and each stage timed to the minute. The aims of the lesson must be precisely spelt out, typically with a linguistic focus and in terms of predicted achievements, as in: 'By the end of the lesson, learners will have learnt the future perfect, and will be able to use it to talk about their hopes for the future.'

All this, of course, runs counter to Dogme principles. In an unplugged approach, no amount of pre-planning can predict – to the letter – what will actually happen on the day. The lesson plan can only be a rough sketch, therefore: more like the agenda for a meeting, or a flow-chart of multiple-branching possibilities. In a Dogme approach, the linguistic outcomes cannot be exactly specified, and certainly not in terms of what learners will have learned.

Learning – especially language learning – is not a linear, uniform, incremental, nor easily measurable process. It is idiosyncratic, recursive, capricious and essentially messy. It may proceed in sudden leaps of understanding, followed by relatively long periods of stasis, even of backsliding. And every learner will do it differently. So to try and impose a timetable on it, with all the punctuality of a Swiss train, is a recipe for disappointment.

Implications

What can a teacher hope to demonstrate in an assessed, and unplugged, lesson? Well, for a start, the teacher is the person in the room who is best equipped to *create the conditions* of learning. There is insufficient space here to detail what these are (but see Part A of *Teaching Unplugged* for a longer discussion). Nevertheless, and in a nutshell, we can aspire to a lesson:

- where maximum opportunities for meaningful, creative and interactive language use are generated;
- where the learners' attention is periodically directed to features of linguistic form;
- where these processes are supported by a relaxed but engaged classroom dynamic.

Teaching an observed lesson

This is more likely to foster learning than a lesson where these conditions are not met. Dogme would seem to offer plenty of scope here. Moreover, the teacher is well-placed to be able to orchestrate and balance, moment by moment, the multiple demands of the complex classroom ecology.

Nothing impresses an examiner more than the teacher's ability to think on the spot, to deal with problems, to exploit the unexpected, to distribute their attention generously, to validate the contribution of each individual learner, and to be alert to emergent learning opportunities. Again, the Dogme lesson – not shackled to a rigid lesson plan or pre-specified language aims – frees teachers to *demonstrate* the in-flight skills that really support learning.

Indications

- Try it out first! Even though this is experimental practice, it shouldn't be so innovative that you might come across to the assessor as simply trying it out and seeing what happens.
- Show that even if the lesson is not planned in detail, you are prepared for all contingencies. This is the difference between '*preparing* a lesson' and '*being prepared* for a lesson'. A lesson plan in the form of a map with multiple routes may be one way of assuring your examiner that you have thought it through.
- Demonstrate that the lesson is not simply a 'one-off' – but that it forms part of a sequence, and that what happens in this lesson will provide material for the next.
- Make reasonable predictions about linguistic outcomes, without necessarily specifying achievable linguistic aims. If, for example, you wish to stimulate a discussion about a forthcoming event, such as an election, it's reasonable to suppose that the language of futurity and of possibility will come up. The ability to predict emergent language is a measure of your experience as a reflective teacher.
- Relax the learners into the lesson (remember: they are being 'observed', too!) by starting with a straight-forward activity that has them interacting in pairs or small groups immediately. Eliciting ideas from the class when everyone is feeling a bit nervous is probably not the best way to start an observed lesson.
- Don't expect a lesson that took off in one direction with one class to do exactly the same with another. Think of the lesson like a chess game or a football match where – even when all the starting conditions are the same – the actual outcome is entirely different each time.

In short ...
An experienced teacher trainer and examiner once told us that the true test of a teacher would be to hand over a used bus ticket fifteen minutes before the observed lesson, and say: 'Base the lesson entirely on this'. He was only half joking!

Teaching unplugged for a term

If you are encouraged by your experience of unplugged lessons, you may want to see whether there is longevity in the approach. Can it be stretched beyond a small number of lessons and used across a term, during a whole course – even for a whole year?

To some extent, a natural cycle emerges from regular use of the teaching techniques outlined in Teaching Unplugged. *This involves uncovering language and discussing it in class, then using techniques to explore and extend language use, and then finally building in recall.*

Using a range of activities and using a variety of small-scale stimulus to introduce different text types will help to sustain the 'long conversation' that is a Dogme class. But there are other strategies you can adopt to help ensure the process goes smoothly.

Issues

Coursebooks are specifically designed to be used on a regular basis. This is one reason they are used in schools. While this can mean an overly-controlled approach, it does ensure that the lesson doesn't run away from the participants.

The more independent of coursebook and external syllabus your teaching becomes, the more important it is to obtain feedback from your class on what they find *enjoyable* and what they find *useful*. It is important to be prepared for what may well be 'teething problems' as you introduce new ways of teaching: some learners may be used to different styles, or uncertain as to where the classes are headed.

And however encouraging your experience in your own classes, you may feel isolated in your place of work. You may even be under pressure to conform to an established way of teaching.

Implications

Unplugged teaching is highly responsive and draws on language from the learners' everyday experience, but it is still possible, and even desirable, to introduce an element of routine into your lessons. Provided an activity is enjoyable and can be varied sufficiently, people will enjoy doing it *regularly*.

Once you have tried a number of unplugged activities and have a sense of which are working well with a class, you can start to *timetable* the most successful ones. This will help you to establish a basic routine, with stepping stones across the week (and the weeks) which you can all look forward to. This will also help to give your class a kind of rhythm, reinforcing the natural cycle of emergent language we have been outlining. You can include your learners in this process by inviting them to discuss the activities they have enjoyed and not enjoyed, and the ones they would most like to repeat in the following week.

It is helpful to be able to share with your class and colleagues your reasons for teaching in this way, but perhaps the most persuasive thing of all is the motivating impact of so much language that is relevant to the learners, clarified by a focus on form in which they are *active participants*.

Teaching unplugged for a term

Indications

- Once you have a real-life context to work with, think of different angles from which it can be approached, and different tasks which can be used to generate and practise relevant language. (For example, a student complains during a break about a biscuit he has bought. A trivial incident. But taking it and 'running with it', you set up a 'taste test' with different food stuffs to generate lexical sets to do with flavour and (personal) taste. In the next lesson, the class work on a letter complaining about the biscuit, which is sent to the manufacturer. When a reply arrives from the biscuit company, you analyse the letter. Other tasks, such as roleplays and telephone routines, can be interpolated into a situation of this sort.)
- The real example above, which involves sending off for authentic information, can create a sense of suspense that stretches between lessons. Speed the process up if you have e-mail: there are all sorts of enquiries that will generate a reply.
- Set up a simple feedback loop. You can do this by preparing a feedback-form template which can be copied from the board by the learners. It might have four headings, such as:
  - What I enjoyed this week
  - What I didn't enjoy so much
  - What was useful to me
  - What was less useful to me
- People can fill out their forms individually and share their feedback with a partner before handing them in to you. After collecting in the sheets, you read them through and give feedback to the whole class. You can also arrange one-to-one feedback sessions.
- Homework can be open-ended as well as specific. 'Noticing' language is a critical step in the learning process; and the more you involve your class in sourcing language and sharing their observations, the better. Depending on the number of English speakers where you are teaching, this can be done online, or on the bus. Encourage your class to make notes of what they read and hear outside class, and set aside time at the beginning of each lesson so they can share what they have noted and ask you any questions they may have.
- 'Stuff happens', as we know only too well. Keep a record that can be followed up by anyone teaching your class if you are absent for any reason. This will help to satisfy the logistical demands of your colleagues and course director.

In short ...

Be prepared for setbacks as well as exciting discoveries: learn from your mistakes and make a record of what works in what context. Share your experience with other teachers who are interested in teaching unplugged, and don't shy away from feedback from colleagues who *aren't* convinced.

It's only by working through the relevance of this approach to your own teaching context that you can make it work there. Dogme isn't a set of rules, it's an example of emergent, shared practice, to which you contribute.

Unplugging a school

Our final 'teaching focus' centres on managing change within an English department or perhaps a even whole school.

Proposing to 'unplug' on a wider scale involves a major culture shift that will affect everyone, from teachers and learners to managers and administrators. It isn't something that can be done overnight, and it isn't something that can be done by decree.

Successful teachers achieve results in many different ways, and it's vital to be flexible when it comes to extending Dogme – in fact, to be non-dogmatic!

Issues and implications

There are a number of possible reasons for taking on the challenge of unplugging a whole school or a language department. One is *conviction*, because we believe that this is the best way to meet the language learning needs of our learners. Another may be *commercial*: we sense that the 'market' is ready for a different approach, and that a promise to focus primarily on learner interests and language will prove attractive.

These reasons are not incompatible, and may also dovetail with a third, which suggests itself strongly at the time of writing *Teaching Unplugged*. With headlines like 'Western financial crisis turns global' and fears that the world economy is heading for prolonged recession, it may not be too fanciful to suggest that an approach that uses fewer resources – less paper on a grand scale, less technology, less electricity even – may have some appeal to schools. And did anyone mention the environment?

Managing change is difficult in any organisation (it is difficult enough in our own lives!) – and a school is no exception. For example, one of the ironies of teaching is that, although we work together with learners, we often work in isolation from our colleagues. Very often, we are observed only when our own performance, or that of the school, is being assessed. This can lead to teachers feeling tense about the idea of sharing classroom ideas where they are most immediate – in the classroom itself. This is just one of the challenges we can face if we want to change the culture of a school: there are barriers to be broken down that have nothing to do with methodology.

- If you are a teacher yourself, advocating change may be easier, as you will be able to lead by example.
- If you are not a teacher, but are still enthused by the ideas in *Teaching Unplugged*, having at least one member of staff who is passionate and articulate about unplugged possibilities will be invaluable.

Whatever your aims, it is vital to discuss the approach you want to take with as many stakeholders as possible – and to manage change, as far as you can, in the way that you propose to teach: *by talking to people*!

Talking about teaching

From a teaching point of view, one is tempted to say that the answer is: training, training, training. But it isn't quite that simple, and 'training', in any case, feels too top-down to achieve the kind of peer advocacy that is essential to achieving meaningful change. A better touchstone for change might be *sharing*.

Unplugging a school

- Routinely sharing access to one another's classrooms will remove the tension from peer observation and make it much easier to share ideas. Start with your own lessons: encourage people to 'drop in', and invite feedback.
- Set up a 'panel' including administrators, teachers and learners, to provide regular feedback on how unplugged ideas are working in practice.
- Share both positive and negative feedback with colleagues in a semi-formal environment, such as voluntary but timetabled and advertised weekly sessions for staff. Share teaching tips and techniques in regular workshop sessions. This will ensure that doubts are aired and discoveries captured.
- Introduce *imaginative* timetabling – rather than dividing classes by 'level', label classrooms by theme, using topics chosen by the learners, and let the learners decide what they are most interested in exploring. These themes might relate to language areas, or to topics. And allow for *looser* timetabling – permitting learners to move between classes when they want to.
- Open up the classrooms. The idea of teachers and learners sitting in on each other's classes can only really take off if there is open access; and if there is a little extra noise, it will replicate normal language processing conditions.
- Open up the staffroom: a *shared* social place, with a library of English language reference books, newspapers and magazines, will represent better use of space, and a surer embodiment of unplugged values.
- Give up the photocopier. The waste is colossal, the stress considerable, and the benefit to learners minimal.
- Order only a minimum of resource books, and ensure that as many of these as possible are books that can be used by both staff and learners, such as learner dictionaries and reference books.

Talking about training

- Teaching is both a skill and an art – like learning to drive or to play the guitar. Or like learning English as a second language, for that matter. It is generally accepted that artistry is best developed through practice. And that declarative knowledge (*knowledge-that*) needs to become procedural knowledge (*knowledge-how*) if the practitioner is ever going to be able to perform fluidly in real-time conditions.
- The principle that Dogme is less about materials reduction, and more about learner-centred, experiential learning, applies equally to teacher training. There is no point in artificially reducing your materials if that is going to limit your effectiveness as a trainer.
- The trainer who professes a low-tech, trainee-centred 'Dogme approach' and yet consistently uses elaborate Powerpoint presentations, reinforced with copious photocopied handouts, is clearly in danger of a loss of credibility. And yet, isn't training different to teaching? Isn't there a body of knowledge – about learning and about language – that needs to be transmitted, and shouldn't it therefore be transmitted using *any means available*, preferably those with the most impact?
- This is the dilemma the Dogme trainer faces, whether training at in-service level or at pre-service level; whether teaching graduate or post-graduate classes; whether training on extended courses or conducting short one-off workshops.
- However, experimenting with extreme privation from time to time can help to concentrate the mind amazingly. As in teaching, it is an affirming experience to find out how much you can rely on the learners to do the teaching for you. And think what a great example you are setting!

- It is axiomatic that teacher trainers should set a good example to their trainees, both in terms of their classroom management skills and in the way they engage their trainees with the content of their programme.
- Teacher training without teaching practice – whether peer teaching, micro-teaching, team-teaching, or some kind of apprenticeship – is unlikely to have any long-term impact on the trainee. And most trainees on programmes where there is an embedded practicum attest to the fact that it was during the practicum, and the feedback that they received, that their real learning kicked in.
- It is less clear, we would argue, that 'delivery' is always the most effective or the most appropriate mode for teacher training.
- There is no real reason why this hands-on approach can't extend to 'theory' sessions as well. Or that the 'delivery' of course content can't (at least sometimes) be mediated outside the classroom, using the wide range of technological means (the internet, e-mail) now available. Not to mention the use of books – like *Teaching Unplugged*!
- You can post your notes and handouts on a dedicated course website, by means of an online learning management system such as Moodle or online discussion forums such as Yahoo Groups; or simply by e-mailing then to your trainees, using a group address. Summaries of your sessions can be posted, using the same means. You might also assign trainees, working in rotation, the job of posting session summaries themselves.

From a training point of view, then, teacher development is like learner development: it is an organic process that flourishes best in conditions where a sense of community encourages the free exchange of ideas. If technology can be enlisted to further this exchange, so much the better. But if it is being used simply because it's there, then maybe it should be unplugged.

Finally ...

Many of the ideas outlined above may draw a response of: 'fine in theory ... !' from readers working in all but the most independent reaches of the private sector. The notion of recasting your school as an 'unplugged' institution may lie beyond your sphere of influence, whatever your personal instincts.

But tides turn in education, as in the global economy. Testing and measurement have become increasingly central to the way we teach and thus to the way we bring up our children, but even the most fiercely defended systems can crumble. In the UK, some of the tests introduced for schoolchildren have just been abandoned, partly in response to reports finding that they distort education (encouraging 'teaching to the test') and contribute to a 'pervasive anxiety' in the lives of children.

The 'testing economy' includes coursebooks and published materials (on shelves and online) that reflect and promote a reductive, one-piece-at-a-time approach to teaching and learning. It is the testing economy that allows teachers to sanction online homework for learners that involves clicking dully on multiple-choice questions until they arrive at the right answer. 'Unplugging' means challenging that economy, and restoring to the classroom the human curiosity and exchange that lies at the heart of learning. One lesson at a time, one school at a time? We won't know unless we try.

From the editors

Teaching Unplugged is the first book to deal comprehensively with the approach in English Language Teaching known as Dogme ELT. It challenges not only the way you view *teaching*, but also the way you view *being a teacher*.

Dogme ELT has been in existence as such for some years now, emerging from a series of articles and evolving into a vibrant online discussion. It advocates teaching 'unplugged': a materials-light, conversation-driven philosophy of teaching that, above all, focuses on the learner and on emergent language.

- A background to the ideas behind teaching unplugged.
- A detailed explanation of the core principles behind Dogme ELT.
- The situation of the approach within the history of foreign language teaching.
- An invitation to reflect on the best way to learn a language and, consequently, to teach it.

- A bank of activities that teachers can use right away and which help them 'unplug their teaching' from the start.
- Activities that involve little or no preparation, often requiring no more than pen, paper and the people in the room.
- Thought-provoking rationales, with easy-to-follow procedures and follow-up.
- Tips, techniques and key terms to facilitate a new approach to teaching.

- Who can teach unplugged?
- Where can Dogme ELT be applied (from the young learner classroom to English for Specific Purposes)?
- What are the issues and implications when adopting a new style of teaching: from accommodating a coursebook to unplugging a whole school?
- How can some insightful indications help?

In short, *Teaching Unplugged* represents an exciting new chapter in alternative and progressive educational theory. We believe it stands out in that it not only explains what this new kind of teaching is, but also how teachers can begin adapting their practice accordingly, in a manner that is both accessible and enjoyable.

Mike Burghall
Lindsay Clandfield

From the publisher

DELTA TEACHER DEVELOPMENT SERIES

A pioneering new series of books for English Language Teachers
with professional development in mind.

The Developing Teacher
by Duncan Foord
ISBN 978-1-905085-22-4

Teaching Unplugged
by Luke Meddings and Scott Thornbury
ISBN 978-1-905085-19-4

For details of future titles in the series, please contact the publisher or visit
the DTDS website at www.deltapublishing.co.uk/DTDS

Also from DELTA PUBLISHING

professional perspectives

A series of practical methodology books designed to provide teachers of English
with fresh insights, innovative ideas and original classroom materials.

Creating Conversation in Class
by Chris Sion
ISBN 978-0-953309-88-7

Talking Business in Class
by Chris Sion
ISBN 978-1-900783-64-4

Challenging Children
by Henk van Oort
ISBN 978-1-900783-93-4

The MINIMAX Teacher
by Jon Taylor
ISBN 978-0953309-89-4

Dealing with Difficulties
by Luke Prodromou and Lindsay Clandfield
ISBN 978-1-905085-00-2

The Resourceful English Teacher
by Jonathan Chandler and Mark Stone
ISBN 978-0-953309-81-8

Humanising your Coursebook
by Mario Rinvolucri
ISBN 978-0-954198-60-2

Unlocking Self-expression through NLP
by Judith Baker and Mario Rinvolucri
ISBN 978-1-900783-88-0

Spontaneous Speaking
by David Heathfield
ISBN 978-1-900783-92-7

Using the Mother Tongue
by Sheelagh Deller and Mario Rinvolucri
ISBN 978-0-954198-61-9

Please contact the publisher for further details:
Tel +44 (0)1306 731770   *E-mail* info@deltapublishing.co.uk
Web www.deltapublishing.co.uk
